FASCINATING

TRUE
TALES FROM
OLD
CALIFORNIA

**CROOKED CON MEN,
ECCENTRIC IMMIGRANTS,
AND FEARLESS FEMALES
WHO SHAPED THE GOLDEN STATE**

COLLEEN ADAIR FLIEDNER

TWODOT®

ESSEX, CONNECTICUT
HELENA, MONTANA

T0283891

A · TWODOT® · BOOK

An imprint of Globe Pequot, the trade division of
The Rowman & Littlefield Publishing Group, Inc.
4501 Forbes Blvd., Ste. 200
Lanham, MD 20706

Distributed by NATIONAL BOOK NETWORK

British Library Cataloguing in Publication Information available

Library of Congress Cataloging-in-Publication Data

Names: Fliedner, Colleen Adair, author.
Title: Fascinating true tales from old California : crooked con men, eccentric immigrants, and fearless females who shaped the Golden State / Colleen Adair Fliedner.
Other titles: Crooked con men, eccentric immigrants, and fearless females who shaped the Golden State
Description: Essex, Connecticut : Two Dot, [2023] | Includes bibliographical references and index. | Summary: "In Fascinating True Tales from Old California, author Colleen Adair Fliedner mines the history of the Golden State to collect more than forty tales of famous Californians and their escapades from 1542 through 1940. Readers will be entertained and enlightened as they take a trip through California's colorful past"—Provided by publisher.
Identifiers: LCCN 2022040822 (print) | LCCN 2022040823 (ebook) | ISBN 9781493063239 (paperback) | ISBN 9781493063246 (epub)
Subjects: LCSH: California—History—Anecdotes. | California—Biography—Anecdotes.
Classification: LCC F861.6 .F55 2023 (print) | LCC F861.6 (ebook) | DDC 979.4—dc23/eng/20220824
LC record available at https://lccn.loc.gov/2022040822
LC ebook record available at https://lccn.loc.gov/2022040823

∞™ The paper used in this publication meets the minimum requirements of American National Standard for Information Sciences—Permanence of Paper for Printed Library Materials, ANSI/NISO Z39.48-1992.

Contents

CONTENTS

Author's Notes

FASCINATING TRUE TALES FROM OLD CALIFORNIA: CROOKED CON MEN, Eccentric Immigrants, and Fearless Females Who Shaped the Golden State contains a sampling of the lives of many of the most interesting people who were part of California's colorful history. Selecting the stories to include in the book was difficult, as there are hundreds from which to choose. In the end, I decided to write a cross-section of stories that might be unfamiliar to many of my readers, like why ladybugs are considered lucky, California's participation in the Civil War, the pirate attack in Monterey, the only woman who was hanged in California, and much more. Included are biographies about some of the state's most amazing movers and shakers, like James Lick, Leland Stanford, and John Downey, all famous names to Californians. Some of the topics are fun and light, while others are heavy and serious. My goal was to include something for everyone to enjoy, and to teach, entertain, and surprise you. For most readers, many of these narratives will make you say, *"Wow! I didn't know that!"*

I wrote each of these chapters as a stand-alone story. That way, they don't need to be read in any sort of order. The problem is that putting the book together in this way creates some duplication of information, such as the introductions for stories taking place during the gold rush. I've also included references in parentheses to other chapters in the book that are relevant to the chapter being read. That way, readers can find additional information on that topic. I hope this "cross-pollination" helps you get the biggest possible picture of the events I'm describing.

Since so many people in these stories lived in the same place and at the same time, they would have either known each other or have been affected by each other's actions. For example, the social elite, most of whom had become millionaires from the gold rush, probably attended the same balls and theater performances, dined at the same fine restaurants, went to the same churches, and shopped at the same stores. The more prominent men would have likely known each other through their membership in the Masons or other organizations. Their experiences, their children's time at school, everything in their lives would have intersected and overlapped, especially in Northern California's earliest days.

I've included a timeline of many of the major events that occurred in California between 1542 and the early part of the twentieth century to help you reference and understand the complicated patchwork of history in the Golden State.

As for me, I was born and raised in California. I studied history and anthropology in college, with a specialization in California history. And I worked as a research historian for the California University system, conducting oral history interviews and research grants relating to California history. Through the years, I've collected a vast library of old and new California history books, and I've spent years traveling around the state visiting most of the places I've written about in this book.

I hope you enjoy reading these stories as much as I've loved researching and writing them. If you have any questions, please contact me at my website: colleenadairfliedner.com. While there, you can click on my blog to read more interesting stories on various historical topics.

Introduction

TODAY'S CALIFORNIA IS A COLLAGE OF CUSTOMS, RELIGIONS, ETHNICI-ties, and beliefs. Even its geography is so varied that it has five different climate zones. Encompassing 163,696 square miles, nearly forty million people, 840 miles of coastline, and eleven major ports, California ranks fifth in the world's economy and the first in the United States. Indeed, it could be its own country.

California's beginnings were quite humble. There weren't any pilgrims landing on its shores. Nor was California part of the Colonies that fought against the English for America's sovereignty. In fact, it wasn't even part of the United States until 1850. Prior to that, it had been a Spanish territory that was taken over by Mexico in 1821. According to historical records, the territory was poorly managed by more than forty governors during the twenty-five years it was under Mexican rule. What was then called Alta (Upper) California was basically left in the hands of its residents, consisting of the Mexican and Spanish settlers; a handful of transplanted Americans, many who married into wealthy Mexican families that owned vast ranchos; and what was left of the local Native American tribes.

A war between Mexican and American forces to determine the fate of the southwestern territories, including California, occurred from 1846 to 1848. As a result of the American victory, the impatient Anglos in California didn't wait for a formal invitation to make California a state. Instead, they drafted their own constitution and petitioned for statehood almost before the ink had dried on the official documents with Mexico.

It was inevitable the United States government would welcome California and its newfound wealth into its fold once they had learned about the discovery of gold on the American River. Thus, California became the thirty-first state on September 9, 1850.

Because California was isolated by mountain ranges, the Pacific Ocean, and vast deserts, it was a difficult place to reach. Still, when the Argonauts (men on a quest to find gold) heard the siren's call proclaiming gold had been found in the Sierra Nevada Mountains, tens of thousands of them traveled to the "Golden State" by wagon or by ship. It was a long and dangerous journey, no matter which mode of transportation they took.

Thousands died along the way. Exhaustion, disease, starvation, accidents, and even Indian attacks made the prospect of going to California frightening and daunting. And yet, the hopefuls continued to come, risking everything to live their dreams. Perhaps they would become rich in the mines and then return to their homes on the East Coast, or Europe, or South America, or the British Isles. Some planned to stay in California, where they could use their newfound wealth to buy cheap land for farming.

Of course, just as happened elsewhere in America, the Native people were the losers in the repopulation of California. Under Spanish rule, they had been rounded up and made to work for the Franciscan padres. They were used for labor, building the missions, raising crops for the padres, growing grapes, and producing wine.

The Native tribes didn't fare any better during the years Mexico ran the territory. But things went from bad to worse when California became a state and its first American governor came into power. Indigenous people were hunted and killed by marauding gangs, who were paid by California's Anglo government to eliminate them. Most of those who survived were made to live on reservations, while their tribal lands were gobbled up by the newly arrived residents.

When California was granted statehood, it changed the course of American history. No other state had ever received such world fame as California. There were those who actually made their fortune in the mines. For most, however, their time spent in the Sierra Nevada Mountains, in what was called the Mother Lode country, there was disappointment, sickness, and even death.

While some returned to their home countries or states, many of those weary souls decided to stay. Stories abound about the men who gave up on finding the elusive gold and opened a mercantile, drug store, hotel, or some other type of business, thus making their fortunes by "mining the miners." More often than not, the people who had migrated to California to search for gold had spent their last dollar just getting there. With broken bodies and empty pocketbooks, there was no way for them to pay for a return journey home. They wandered the city streets, turned to alcohol, and often died far from their families.

During the Mexican period, California, and especially Southern California, had become a patchwork of grand cattle ranches (called *ranchos*). Famous for their festivals, hospitality, and vaqueros (horsemen), the ranchos finally disappeared after a lengthy drought in the early 1860s, resulting in the death of the vast cattle herds. The drought was the death knell for the ranchos, causing most of the owners to declare bankruptcy when they were unable to pay back loans they had taken against their property. And there were plenty of eager bankers, like John Downey, ready to foreclose on their ranchero friends to take the land for themselves. New developments sprang up where cattle had once roamed, and the vast open landscape began to be covered with towns, houses, fences, and roads.

And Old California was gone.

Today, California is the most populated state in the Union. With its tossed salad of humanity and an abundance of opportunities for almost everyone, the state has developed its own personality and an undeniable sense of independence.

Brief California History Timeline

SPANISH PERIOD (1769–1821)

1542	Cabrillo claims California for Spain.
1741	Russians establish a trading post in Sitka, Alaska.
July 1769	Father Junipero Serra dedicates the first mission in San Diego. Another twenty missions will be built north of San Diego between 1769 and 1823, ending with Mission San Francisco Solano.
October 1769	Gaspar de Portola leads an exploratory march from San Diego, north to what is now Monterey.
June 1770	Monterey is officially founded and serves as the first capital of Alta California under both Spanish and Mexican rule.
June 1776	Mission Dolores is built at San Francisco de Asis in honor of St. Francis of Assisi.
Fall 1781	Forty-four men, women, and children are the first settlers to arrive at the new pueblo of Los Angeles. Led by a detachment of seventeen Spanish soldiers, they consist of eleven married couples and twenty-two children. Most are of mixed race: mestizo, black, Indian, and Spanish.
1785–1846	The Spanish government awards large parcels of land to retiring soldiers as an incentive to keep them from leaving Alta California. After Mexico takes ownership of the territory, the government continues giving land grants to citizens of Mexico to encourage them to move to California to raise cattle and resume the process of settling the sparsely populated areas.

1812   The Russians establish Fort Ross near what is now Bodega Bay north of San Francisco. They grow food for the fur trappers and soldiers, including sending food by ship to their settlements in Alaska. The Russian American Fur Company hunts otters and sends their skins back to their home country. Spain sees the Russian settlement as a threat to its claim on California and deepens its need to populate the region to keep it as a Spanish colony.

MEXICAN PERIOD (1821–1846)

1821   Mexico's independence from Spain includes taking over Alta California. Missions are secularized, and the mission system slowly disintegrates over the next decade.

1824   The Mexican Colony Law is passed by the Mexican government, establishing new rules for gifting large parcels of land in Alta California.

1828   More than thirty land grants have already been awarded to Spanish soldiers under Spanish colonial rules. The Mexican Colony Law breaks up the enormous parcels of land that had formerly been granted to the twenty-one missions and allows Mexican citizens, most of whom are relatives or friends of Mexican officials, to petition for the newly available acreage. The original promise Mexico had made was that the land would be returned to the Indigenous tribes who had occupied those areas for generations. That promise was broken, and the Indians who had survived diseases introduced by the European and American settlers were subjugated to working as servants or laborers, while others were forced to live on reservations.

1834	Mexicans living in California demand that the vast amount of property given to the missions when they were established—literally owned by the Catholic Church—be taken back by the Mexican government. This results in the "Decree of Confiscation," which allows Mexican residents to purchase the newly available lands at cheap prices.
1839	The first land grant given to a non-Mexican is awarded to John Sutter. Sutter's Fort was near what would become the town of Sacramento. Its original name was "New Helvetia," after Sutter's homeland in Switzerland. Sutter grows crops that are sold to immigrants arriving via wagon trains along the California Trail.
1841	John Sutter purchases Fort Ross from the Russians. They abandon the settlement after they have decimated the otter population and their fur trade is ruined.
May 1841	The first overland wagon train of Americans bound for California leaves from Kansas City. Led by the famous John Bidwell, part of the group splits off, heading for Oregon. The rest of the settlers barely survive crossing the eastern Sierra Nevada Mountains.
1842	Gold is found in what is now called Placerita Canyon southwest of the Antelope Valley by Francisco Lopez. While searching for lost cattle in the canyon, he stops to eat lunch by a stream, pulls up a few wild onions, and discovers the shiny flakes on the plant's roots.
1845	As fears of a war with Mexico grow after numerous conflicts in Texas, United States naval ships (the Pacific Squadron) are sent around Cape Horn to patrol California's waters. They are ordered to secure all ports along the coast in the event of war with Mexico.

May 1846	Mexico officially goes to war with the United States.
July 1846	A small group of American settlers, happy to be out from under the control of Mexican officials, declare their own independence from Mexico. Calling themselves "Los Osos," they raise the "Bear Flag of the California Republic" in Sonoma. Their victory is short-lived when John Fremont and his troops arrive and claim California for the United States. The flag adopted for California's eventual statehood, however, includes much of the Bear Flag's design.
August 1846	General John Fremont leads troops into Los Angeles in a parade-like display, complete with a band playing. At that time, Los Angeles is the largest town in Alta California. Mexican generals, including Andres Pico, lead campaigns to reclaim Los Angeles at the Battle of San Pasqual north of San Diego, the Battle of Dominguez Rancho, and the Battle of Rio San Gabriel. Fremont temporarily leaves Los Angeles because his troops are outnumbered.
1846	Yerba Buena (San Francisco's original name) is claimed by the U.S. Navy. The American flag is flown in the town's main plaza.
January 13, 1847	Mexican officials in California (Californios) sign the Treaty of Cahuenga ending the war in Alta California.
1847	The name Yerba Buena is changed to San Francisco.
January 1848	John Marshall discovers gold on the American River.
February 1848	The Treaty of Guadalupe Hidalgo formally ends the war with Mexico in all affected areas: Texas, New Mexico, and the northern portion of California (Alta). Baja California remains under Mexican rule.
January 1849	Shiploads of prospectors from Chile, including Vicente Pérez Rosales, who come to search for gold are among the earliest miners in the goldfields.

Spring 1849	The first wagons with Americans arrive for the gold rush. An estimated twenty-five thousand men, women, and children make the overland trip to California during the early years after the discovery of gold.
August 1849	The first shiploads of gold-seeking hopefuls from America arrive in San Francisco and head for the Mother Lode country in the Sierra Nevada Mountains.
September 1849	A constitution is drafted in Monterey that sets up a state government, even though statehood hasn't yet been granted by Washington, DC.
September 1850	California's statehood is official. San Jose is chosen as the new state capital. A provisional state government is set up with Peter Hardeman Burnett as the first American governor.
1850	Sacramento, which means "sacrament" in Spanish, is incorporated, making it the oldest incorporated city in California. Because of its proximity to the gold-fields, Sacramento becomes a trading and shipping center with a burgeoning population of merchants and their families. It doesn't become the state capital until 1854.
1850–1860	Calling for the extermination of California's Indigenous people, Governor Burnett authorizes groups of private citizens to participate in the killing of Native Americans. The state spends more than $1 million to fund this wholesale bloodbath. The survivors of the more than one hundred tribes are sent to newly created reservations or to work as laborers on ranches.
March 1851	The California Land Act is passed, requiring owners of the vast acreage granted to them under Spanish or Mexican rule to prove legal ownership.
June 1851	A Committee of Vigilance is formed in San Francisco to address violent crimes many residents feel are being ignored by the local government.

1852	The first Wells, Fargo & Company office opens in San Francisco, providing banking and express services.
1853	Levi Strauss arrives in San Francisco from Bavaria, opening a dry goods store. He will eventually create his famous canvas pants with rivets on the pockets for miners.
1854	The American government sets up the San Francisco Mint.
1853–1854	Mare Island Naval Yard is established on San Pablo Bay to support the Pacific Naval Squadron. Commander David Farragut and his family arrive and establish their residence on the island.
January 1855	Panama's new railroad running between the Atlantic and Pacific Oceans is completed, making it much easier for people to get to California.
February 1855	To service the miners in the gold diggings, one of the first railroads in California is constructed between Folsom and Sacramento.
May 1856	A Second Committee of Vigilance is formed in San Francisco, because many people believe there is too much political corruption.
1859	Alcatraz Island Prison is built to incarcerate criminals convicted of serious crimes. During the Civil War, Confederate insurrectionists are also held there.
1861	The Civil War breaks out in South Carolina.
1862	The Great California Drought means the final end of the grand old ranchos.
1865	The Civil War ends.
1868	An earthquake hits, doing substantial damage. It is centered in the East Bay.
1869	John Downey and Phineas Banning establish the first railroad in Southern California between the harbor at Wilmington (formerly known as New San Pedro) and Los Angeles.

1869	The completion of the transcontinental railroad connects Northern California with the rest of the United States. It brings even more immigrants to California.
1870	Golden Gate Park opens in San Francisco.
1870	The total number of all the Native American people in California is estimated to be around 150,000 at the beginning of the gold rush. By 1870, those numbers drop to around 30,000.
1870	Flecks of gold are found in a creek in San Diego County near the small town of Julian.
1871	A racially charged attack in Los Angeles' Chinatown results in the hanging of between seventeen and twenty Chinese men.
1876	The Southern Pacific Railroad linking Northern and Southern California is completed.
1877	Violent attacks on Chinese immigrants in San Francisco leave four Chinese men dead, and a great deal of property in Chinatown is damaged or destroyed.
1880	Scottish writer Robert Louis Stevenson arrives in Monterey, California.
May 1882	The Chinese Exclusion Act prohibits Chinese citizens to continue immigrating to California.
1883	Maria Downey, wife of John Downey, is among those killed in a terrible train wreck in the Tehachapi portion of the Southern Pacific Railroad's tracks.
1892	The Chinese Exclusion Act is renewed and becomes "permanent" in 1902. The act is repealed in 1943, although only a limited number of Chinese are allowed to immigrate per year. This changes again in 1952 with the Immigration and Nationality Act, abolishing racial discrimination.
1898	Another earthquake in the Bay Area causes moderate damage.

AFTER 1900

1904   Early versions of submarine performance tests are held in San Pablo Bay near Mare Island. They're so dangerous that the men onboard must provide a will before the dives.

April 1906   A major earthquake and fire destroys much of San Francisco, killing thousands of people. Other nearby cities also experience damage.

1909   Fort Ross State Historic Park is established.

1914   The Panama Canal opens, making California and the Pacific region much more accessible.

1915   The Panama-Pacific International Exposition is held in San Francisco less than ten years after the city's destruction in the 1906 earthquake.

1915   Charles Hatfield, nicknamed the "Rainmaker," is hired to end San Diego's terrible drought.

July 1916   As the nation prepares in case President Wilson decides to go to war against Germany and its allies, California's own National Guard Machine Gun Company trains in San Rafael for the inevitable call to arms. These men had recently returned from guarding the Mexican border.

April 1917   The United States joins the Allied Forces in World War I.

1917   An explosion set off by a German spy at Mare Island kills six people and injures thirty-eight.

SPANISH ERA

Chapter 1
What's in a Name?

CALIFORNIA. THE NAME EVOKES VISIONS OF BEAUTIFUL BEACHES, PER-fect weather, soaring mountains, and a place where people can get a fresh start in life. California. Where people from all over the world can come to live the American dream.

While most states got their names from Spanish terms, Native American languages, or British royalty, the "Golden State" was named after a fictional woman warrior. According to the old Spanish records, the

Queen Calafia mural at the Mark Hopkins Hotel. PAINTING BY MAYNARD DIXON AND FRANK VON SLOUN (1926).

name, California, first appeared in the sixteenth century book *Las Sergas de Esplandián*. It's a romantic tale about a race of Amazon warrior women who lived on a great island west of India called California. The dark-skinned women wore jewelry made of pure gold and precious stones, and they fed their male children to their pet griffins (mythological beasts).

In his novel, Garci Rodriguez de Montalvo describes the women's ruler, Queen Calafia, as a magnificent pagan huntress who leads her followers to Constantinople to defeat the Christians. They rode their griffins into battle and wielded golden weapons. But in the end, good won over evil. The Amazon women all converted to the true religion, an epic tale reflecting Spain's defeat of the Muslims who had invaded the southern portion of their country.

Linguists have theorized that the novel's author simply made up the word *Calafia*, based on the Arabic word *Khalif* (or Khalifa, the feminine spelling of an Arabic ruler). Some historians have postulated that Hernán Cortés had read the famous novel, and after his defeat of the Aztec empire in 1521, he sent ships from his base in Acapulco on the west coast of Mexico to look for the bejeweled Amazon women in the region called California.

When the Spanish sailors came ashore on the tip of what was eventually called Baja California, they believed the land was an island. There were dark-skinned Natives, though they weren't the statuesque Amazon women described in *Las Sergas de Esplandián*. Still, the men believed they had located the island of riches called California. Under that assumption, the Spaniards searched for the gold and jewels that Rodriguez de Montalvo described in his popular novel. Perhaps his readers, and there were large numbers of them, believed the author had some sort of insight into the magical place, and that much of his book was based on fact. Of course, it wasn't. And yet, even after the Spanish explorers didn't find jewels and gold, the name California stuck . . . and at least part of the legend came true with the eventual discovery of gold all over the new territory.

Although there are several versions of this story, we do know that the term *California* began to show up in documents written by Spanish explorers beginning in 1542, when Juan Rodriquez Cabrillo mentioned it in his journal. In reports written by an assistant to Hernán Cortés between 1550 and 1556, there were three references to a region called California that was actually much larger than today's state of California.

Whether it was a territory of Spain, Mexico, or America, Queen Calafia's California has maintained its age-old moniker. The origin of the state's enchanting name is just one more piece of California's unique and colorful history.

Chapter 2
California's Devilish Fleas

DIARIES AND LETTERS FROM THE LATE 1700S THROUGH THE MID-1800s often made references to California's "devilish" flea problem. Visitors wrote bitter accounts of their experiences, complaining that the fleas of California were as bad as "any of the plagues inflicted by Moses and Aaron" upon the Egyptians. The fleas, said one author, were the "punishments of purgatory," and that he hoped he would never see or feel their prickly bites again.

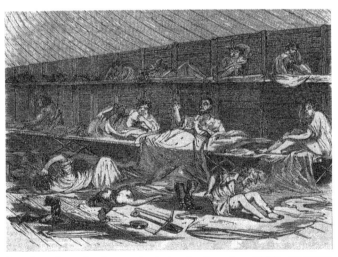

Drawing of guests at a rancho trying to sleep (ca. 1858). COURTESY OF LOS ANGELES PUBLIC LIBRARY.

And yet, the romantic myth of California's ranchos persisted for decades. Tales of beautiful senoritas, dashing vaqueros (horsemen), colorful fiestas, and delicious, spicy foods continued to draw adventurous travelers to Old California. Were reports about the terrible swarms of fleas simply ignored?

The first mention of "California's scourge" was recorded in the diary of Father Juan Crespi in October 1769. Accompanying the first group of Spanish explorers heading north from San Diego, Crespi and the Portola party camped near an abandoned Native American village in the coastal portion of what is now San Mateo County. Curious about how the Indigenous people lived, several soldiers entered one of the "grass habitations." In the dim light, it was hard to see that everything was covered with an undulating layer of fleas. Sensing that a meal had arrived, swarms of the insects began to jump on the poor soldiers. Turning on heel, the men ran from the village, their clothes and flesh crawling with the bloodsuckers.

Naming the area (including much of today's San Mateo County) "Las Pulgas" (the fleas), the expeditioners made a hasty retreat. Today, residents of the area are reminded of Old California's terrible flea problem every time they drive on Alameda de las Pulgas, or Avenue of the Fleas, a busy road that connects many of the cities located within the original 35,240-acre Spanish land grant. The property and adobe house received the unfortunate name "Rancho de las Pulgas."

One adventurer who stayed at a famous rancho in San Bruno Valley (south of San Francisco) was surprised to learn that he would be sleeping with his hosts and their children on a "great leather bed." He said of his experience that each night, they were all "devoured by fleas and badly protected from the evening coolness." It was far from the wonderful experience he had hoped for.

Another group of travelers left a scathing account of their experiences at another rancho. Although the food and entertainment were good, even the nicest buildings were teaming with fleas. The visitors were shocked to discover that scratching (even in the most intimate areas of one's body) was not only socially acceptable but also expected . . . even in mixed company.

The guest house was a small adobe with planks along the walls that served as beds. After entering the building, the men noticed that the floor seemed to be moving. A moment later, the bottoms of their pants were black, their flesh prickling with bites. Hopping up on the "beds" to escape, each man rubbed his lower legs with alcohol, killing enough fleas "to fill a large cemetery." Their efforts were futile. The blankets, the walls, the ceiling—everywhere there was a never-ending supply of hungry fleas. The men sought refuge in a nearby clump of trees. Some slept on piles of boughs, while others climbed into the trees in an effort to catch a few winks. Still, there was no escaping the aggressive parasites, though there were apparently far fewer outside than inside the adobe buildings.

Like the local Native Americans, the Spanish/Mexican population who settled in California had learned to live with the area's flea infestation. Although no one could completely escape the nasty bites, the sun-bronzed skin of the local residents was reputedly far tougher than that of the fair-skinned newcomers. Californios are said to have pitied the "gringos," for they knew that the fleas would be well fed on their tender flesh.

Of course, the "scourge of California" wasn't confined to the ranchos. The mountains of the Sierra Nevada were also breeding grounds for the tiny vampires. An English writer complained that, as soon as he entered his quarters in one of the mining camps, he was attacked by fleas "with a vigor that was perfectly astonishing." He wrote that "unlike most common varieties of flea, the horrible California pests boldly faced their victims as they attacked." He also remarked that the fleas traveled on the ground like "little herds of wild cattle." One can only wonder if this was a slight exaggeration.

The cities didn't fare much better. From Los Angeles to San Francisco, the complaints were the same. For instance, guests staying at the "finest" hotel just south of San Francisco slept on wooden planks covered with blankets that were virtually alive with fleas.

Flea fever, often called "California's epidemic evil," was a common ailment that resulted from infected flea bites. A writer visiting from the East Coast who had contracted the malady said that flea fever "drove away sleep and tormented a man to madness." His tender flesh was covered with oozing red lumps that itched and swelled into a solid mass as a result of hundreds of bites all over his body.

Why was Old California so infested with fleas? Did the fleas come to the area by ship as some people have suggested? Reportedly, there were thousands of rats that jumped from ships docking in the port of San Francisco. And with the rats came millions of fleas. They spread like a prairie fire, living mainly on the blood of wildlife. As time passed and the ranchos' cattle herds multiplied, so did the number of fleas. Though it can't be scientifically proved, the fleas of Old California were supposedly a special variety, "having been weaned on the tough hides of the abundant cattle herds that were raised by the early rancheros." Would that explain why California fleas were especially ravenous and oversized?

Strangest of all, by about 1880, accounts of massive flea attacks all but vanished. When the ranchos and their enormous herds of cattle began to disappear in the 1860s, American farmers planted crops on the land where the cattle once grazed. Hunters killed the local wildlife for food—the same animals on which fleas once fed were served in pots of stew. Cities sprang up where there had once been forests and natural terrain, and the habitat of the flea slowly shrank.

Of course, like every other state, California still has fleas. Thankfully for those of us who live here, they're not as large and numerous as their infamous predecessors.

THE CHAMPION JUMPING FLEA

Miners were an especially grungy bunch, seldom washing their clothes or bathing. Life in the mountains was harsh. The days were long, and the work was grueling. Accommodations were barebones, to say the least. Wood shanties and lean-tos made of tree limbs or oiled cloth were often the only shelter the men had from the cold, pounding rain. The men often spent their nights drinking and gambling in makeshift saloons, where the proprietor simply traded whiskey for the prospector's hard-earned gold. As if conditions weren't miserable enough, the miners' bodies were hosts to countless lice and fleas.

Mark Twain once said, "Never let the truth get in the way of a good story." That's the likely case with this entertaining yarn. Tall tales were often told around campfires at night, a form of entertainment in the otherwise bleak mining camps. This one is about a California gold miner (we'll call him Jed) and his large and rather famous flea (whom we'll call Fred).

As the story goes, Fred was one of many fleas that made their home among Jed's thick chest hair. But Fred was no ordinary flea. The parasite was reportedly quite large and had the ability to jump great heights. Now, you'd think that Jed would have simply smashed the hungry insect. But he hadn't done well with his prospecting and had come up with a brilliant idea. Traveling from camp to camp, he challenged the men to a flea-jumping contest—their best jumper versus Fred.

The other fleas didn't have a chance. Fred became famous for the height and distance he could leap, leaving Jed with far more money than he would have otherwise made panning for gold. The champion flea lived out his short life (six months to a year) in this symbiotic relationship—Fred lived and ate in comfort, while Jed made a small killing in the flea-jumping contests!

Chapter 3
California's Pirate Attack: A Love Story

THE AIR WAS DAMP AND COLD THE AFTERNOON OF NOVEMBER 24, 1818, when the two ships dropped anchor in the bay of Monterey. They didn't fly a flag with a skull and crossbones, and yet, Governor Sola and the Spanish citizens residing in the capital of Alta California had been warned that pirates were headed for the California coast. The ships were under the command of Hipolito (Hypolite) Bouchard, a Frenchman who sailed under the colors of Argentina. One of the ships sailed close

Only known photo of Joseph Chapman and Guadalupe Ortega Chapman (1847).

to shore, as if to taunt the soldiers defending the presidio fortress. The other, larger frigate anchored farther out to sea, out of range for cannon balls to reach.

Pirates on the West Coast? Impossible, or so the Spanish leaders had thought. It was the galleons filled with gold and silver taken from the natives of Central and South America that had been the targets for pirates in the Atlantic as they sailed from the Americas to Spain. And yet, this barely civilized place, this remote seashore along the western territory that still belonged to the Spanish had little to offer in the way of treasure. What, then, were these pirates after?

Spain was now the enemy of Argentina, which had declared its independence from its mother country. Spain's political power and ability to colonize the world was waning, and its treasury was emptier than it had been in more than a century. Was this soon-to-occur invasion by these insurrectionists merely a show of might by Argentina's privateers? Was it a way to harass the Spanish-owned region by sacking its provisional government seat?

As soon as the sails had been spotted on the horizon, the lookouts on Point Pinos sent Governor Sola the news. He evacuated Monterey, leaving a handful of soldiers there to guard the presidio. The few valuable items in town, such as the holy objects in the San Carlos Cathedral, were carted away, far out of reach of the marauders.

Monterey was a town of around three hundred men, women, and children. As was customary for the Spanish when they occupied regions, a presidio or fort had been built to protect the port. Yet, most of the soldiers were gone—off to protect the missions, roadways, and small settlements from bandits and hostile Indigenous people. Those who were left behind guarding Monterey, its presidio, custom house, and church numbered around sixty-five. That wasn't enough to ward off an attack.

As was his usual—or his unusual—habit, Bouchard sent a note ashore to the governor asking him to allow him and his men to occupy the town. He knew he outnumbered the Spanish soldiers and preferred that no blood be spilled. That's how Bouchard earned the nickname "the gentleman captain."

The governor ignored the pirate captain's offer, knowing most of the citizens had evacuated the town. He gathered the important documents from his office and slipped away to hide at a friend's rancho miles from Monterey.

The battle began at sunrise the next morning, November 25, when the commander of the smaller ship, the *Santa Rosa*, began to fire at the buildings in the Royal Presidio. Defenders returned cannon fire, killing five of the sailors on the *Santa Rosa*. In fact, so much damage had been sustained that the remaining crew abandoned the ship, rowing the launches out to Bouchard's ship, the *Argentina*.

By now, the weather had turned foul, and ice-cold rain showered down on the sailors. Hoisting the anchor and unfurling the sails, Bouchard headed west through the storm for a few miles until he found a safe place to land his crew. Between 350 and 400 men—a conglomerate of Argentinians, Kanakas (Hawaiians), Africans, and even a few Americans—made up the invading force. They brought two cannons ashore and traveled through the mud and cold back to Monterey.

Bouchard and his men not only captured the presidio but also burned most of the town. Just a few buildings were left standing, among them San Carlos Cathedral (Bouchard ordered that no one destroy the holy place, or they would be executed) and the customs house where all of the trade goods were loaded and unloaded from merchant ships.

Sailing down the coast to Santa Barbara, Bouchard decided to stop at a small bay next to the Rancho Nuestra Senor del Refugio. Some historians have speculated that the captain saw lights on shore and believed it was Santa Barbara, his next target for pillaging. He sent men ashore, hoping to find more booty than had been gathered in Monterey. What he didn't realize was that he had landed his crew members on Refugio Beach, part of the vast Refugio Rancho, which belonged to the well-known Ortega family.

Another fact that Bouchard didn't know was that the Ortegas had been warned about the approaching pirates by a courier from Monterey, and that they had also evacuated everyone but their vaqueros (cowboys). The pirates burned most of the buildings in retribution for the fact that all of the livestock, including the cattle, had been moved. All the pirates could do was to steal as many food staples, like flour and beans, as they could find. They were also able to fill up their empty water barrels from a nearby stream.

As they were heading back to the beach, the vaqueros, assisted by soldiers who had come to help the Ortegas, attacked. Two men, Joseph Chapman from Boston and an African man named Tom Fisher, were captured and dragged back to the rancho.

Here's where the story becomes more like a romance novel than true history. And yet, this is the story told to author and journalist Harry Carr, who published his book, *Los Angeles*, in 1935. Carr had interviewed countless people who had either lived California's early history or had been born hearing stories from their relatives who had experienced the events that deeply shaped the state. This interview was with the granddaughter of Joseph J. Chapman. Her grandmother was Guadalupe Ortega. In addition, the famous historian Hubert Howe Bancroft conducted countless interviews with the men and women who lived in the mid-to-late 1800s to gather their recollections of their lives in Old California. He, too, tells this story in his papers, now located at the Bancroft Library in Berkeley, California.

The Love Story
Joseph Chapman was born in Boston, Massachusetts, and was trained by his father as a shipbuilder and carpenter. But he was a curious lad, who longed to experience adventure by going to sea. He sailed to the Sandwich Islands (Hawaii) on a cargo vessel but was shanghaied after a night of drinking in Honolulu. When he awoke, he was on one of the two ships commanded by Bouchard, a privateer employed by Argentina. He wasn't mistreated and did what was asked of him, though he had never imagined his situation would become so dire that he had to participate in burning down a town.

When he was ordered to go ashore with his shipmates to sack the Ortega Rancho at Refugio, he didn't object. His life changed in an instant, however, when a group of mounted vaqueros appeared out of nowhere at Rancho Refugio. While wading into the water to climb into a launch boat, he heard a whizzing sound, followed by a tight, burning sensation around his neck. He was pulled backward into the surf, yanking at the braided leather lasso that was strangling him. Choking, breathing in salt water, he lost consciousness.

Joseph came to on the ground. His hands and feet were bound, and he could see he was tied to the tail of a horse. Several vaqueros stood around him, laughing and shouting in Spanish. He would later learn that dragging a man behind a horse was a means of corporal punishment for thieves, and that he was minutes away from dying.

Squinting in the bright sun, he saw a beautiful woman ride up on horseback. She had dark hair and piercing eyes, and her skin almost glowed in the sun. She stared down at him for a long moment, a smile tugging at her lips. Then she shouted something to the vaqueros and rode away. Joseph would later learn her name was Guadalupe Ortega, and that she had ordered him to be spared. She had told the men he had a strong build, and he would be a good asset for helping with construction projects at the Mission Santa Ines (Ynez).

The Spanish speakers gave him the name "El Ingles," meaning "The Englishman," not realizing that he was from Boston and not England. He settled into his new life, and over time, the handsome, burly, blond-haired Bostonian became a novelty. A celebrity of sorts, in fact. His building skills became legendary, and he was sent to various missions to help with projects. One of his specialties was building grist mills, not only for the missions but also for places throughout the Southland, like San Marino.

At least one of the documents about El Ingles relates that his first home was with one of the Lugo families. They treated him kindly, even though he was considered a criminal. Lugo took Joseph to Los Angeles for a while so that he could help with several restoration projects at the San Gabriel Mission. Also, the main church in Los Angeles needed new timbers in its ceiling. Joseph Chapman was a jack-of-all-trades, including, as the story goes, setting broken bones and providing medical aid in the early years before there were doctors in the pueblo.

After Mexico broke away from Spain in 1821 and the mission system no longer existed, Joseph became a Mexican citizen and a free man. He decided he wanted to return to the Central Coast, to the area where he had been captured. Could it have had something to do with the pretty Ortega senorita who had saved his life?

Guadalupe Ortega, daughter of the wealthy rancho owner Jose Francisco Ortega, apparently thought about Joseph as much as he had about her. As time passed, Chapman converted to the Catholic Church. He was baptized and was given the name Jose Juan Chapman. He attended Mass at Santa Ines Mission, where he and Guadalupe saw each other regularly. It wasn't long before Joseph, now Jose, had become so well respected that he was allowed to court Guadalupe. Their love grew, and Guadalupe's father not only gave his consent for their marriage but also gifted the newlyweds their own piece of land. The wedding fiesta lasted for three days of music, dancing, and food with people coming from ranchos and towns all over the region.

Joseph Chapman was now an important and accepted part of local society. In 1822, he moved his family south, living for a time in Los Angeles before purchasing a large ranch from Augustin Machado in what is now Pasadena.

But eventually, Joseph and Guadalupe longed to get back to the Santa Barbara area where much of the Ortega family still resided. It's believed the padres from the Santa Barbara Mission gave Joseph Chapman a large parcel of property near the beach where an old hide house had been built decades earlier to store the cow hides that were once a valued trade item with foreign ship merchants. It was later known as Burton Mound. Some sources say he sold the property, making a handsome profit. He received a square league of land on the Santa Clara River in the San Pedro colony, which was located about ten miles east of Mission San Buenaventura.

The man who was once called a pirate had become a highly respected, wealthy Mexican citizen. Joseph Chapman, known as "El Ingles" for much of his life, died in 1849 and was (and still is) buried in the cemetery at Santa Barbara Mission. Joseph and Guadalupe had eleven children and a long and very happy marriage.

TRUTH OR FICTION

There are many versions of the story of Joseph and Guadalupe's meeting and marriage. One rather outrageous version says Chapman was a large, violent man who found the beautiful Guadalupe praying in the chapel at Refugio while the rancho was being burned by Bouchard and his pirates. Chapman threatened to kill her, but instead he used his torch to burn off one of her braids.

Guadalupe, a sort of Wonder Woman, ran and mounted a waiting horse, riding into Santa Barbara and even to Los Angeles to warn everyone there were pirates heading south to raid these towns. When she and Joseph finally met again years later, he revealed that he had instantly fallen in love with her, taking her burned-off braid to remember her by. He opened his shirt to show her he always wore it around his neck. And then they were married.

BOUCHARD AND THE PIRATES

While it's doubtful Senorita Ortega rode her horse to warn the people of Santa Barbara about Bouchard, it's true the people of Los Angeles were warned in time to protect the town from an attack. But it never happened. The records show that while Bouchard's ships were anchored in San Pedro Bay, he learned the Pueblo of Los Angeles was about twenty-five dusty miles inland. Thus, he decided to skip the travails of marching to Los Angeles. Besides, he had plenty of water and food from the raid on Rancho Refugio.

Bouchard did raid the Mission San Juan Capistrano on December 15, 1818. Again, the padre at the mission had been warned, and roughly one thousand local residents, most of whom were Native people who had been taken to live at the mission, walked eight miles up Trabuco Creek to stay at the Rancho Trabuco for safety. Valuables from the mission were hidden before the pirates came to shore. What the crew members did find were dried beef (jerky) and food staples. And, above all, they raided the padres' wine cellar. The captain discouraged drunkenness, but his men had been on the water for too long, and this was their last stop. Once they returned to the ships, however, the men who had behaved badly, who hadn't followed orders, and who had imbibed until they were sloppy and out of control were flogged.

The small force of Mexican soldiers who had watched the raid from a hill overlooking the town heaved a huge sigh of relief when they saw the two ships hoist their sails and head into the wind. There had been some fires set, some things destroyed inside the church. But Bouchard was gone, and the mission could be rebuilt.

Bouchard sailed back to Argentina empty handed. He continued his life at sea but was killed by one of his servants in Peru in 1837 . . . an ignominious end to the only pirate/privateer captain to ever attack the coastal towns of Old California.

Chapter 4

Catalina Island: Buried Treasures, Mines, and the House of Mirrors

BEFORE THE WATERS BETWEEN SOUTHERN CALIFORNIA AND THE Channel Islands had been accurately charted, dozens of ships wound up ensnared on hidden shoals or rock outcroppings. One of those lost ships was named the *Danube*, which was wrecked off the coast at Point Fermin during a storm in 1824. The crew managed to swim to shore, despite the huge swells and pounding surf.

Here's where the story gets strange. Reportedly, the survivors made their way from San Pedro to San Gabriel Mission, a journey of about thirty-five miles, to get help. Logically, the pueblo of Los Angeles would have been a much closer destination for the wet and exhausted men to seek help. And yet, as the story goes, the men eventually reached the mission, where they found food and shelter.

Samuel Prentiss, one of the sailors who survived the accident, befriended an elderly island chief, Turei (or Turie), who had been the chief of the Pumumbi Ranchero on Santa Catalina Island. Turei and his people had been relocated to the San Gabriel Mission in 1823. Turei suddenly became quite ill. From his deathbed, the old chief told Prentiss about a buried treasure on Catalina and gave him a crudely drawn map of its location. It wasn't clear exactly what the treasure consisted of, but Prentiss believed it was either pieces of eight or gold articles that thieves had plundered from the missions in 1804. Turei said that, before they left

Catalina, his tribe had found the treasure and buried it at the base of a tree for safekeeping. The map literally had an "X marks the spot" on it.

Immediately returning to where his ship had been wrecked, Prentiss salvaged some of the debris, built a small boat, and sailed for Catalina Island. Then bad luck struck. When he was caught in a severe northeaster and nearly capsized, most of his gear, including the infamous map, was washed overboard.

Fortunately, he survived and eventually made it to Catalina. But he wasn't familiar with the island's terrain, and because he no longer had the map, Prentiss only had a vague idea about where to search for the treasure. Building a shanty on the hill overlooking beautiful Emerald Bay, he spent the next thirty years scouring Catalina in search of the elusive treasure. According to the legend, he died in 1854 without ever finding it.

A plaque was constructed overlooking Emerald Bay to commemorate Samuel Prentiss, Catalina's first "white resident." He also holds the dubious honor of being the first white man to die on the island.

Another survivor of the *Danube* shipwreck and a friend of Samuel Prentiss was a Frenchman named Louis Bouchette. Like Prentiss, Bouchette decided to stay in Southern California. Like all good Frenchmen, he loved wine. After marrying a Los Angeles woman, Bouchette purchased a vineyard and went into the wine-making business.

Because of their friendship, Prentiss and Bouchette had stayed in close touch, traveling between the island and the mainland. Louis Bouchette's son, Santos, must have been very close to Prentiss, for on a visit to Los Angeles shortly before he died, Prentiss told young Santos the story of the treasure.

When news of Prentiss's death reached the Bouchette family, Santos immediately set sail for Catalina with grand ideas of wealth swirling in his head. Living in Prentiss's old cabin, he spent years digging holes around every tree he could locate. For decades, some of these holes could still be seen in Cherry Valley, Emerald Bay, and Fourth of July Harbor.

While Santos didn't locate the buried treasure, he discovered a valuable silver lode in Cherry Valley near Emerald Bay in 1860. Returning to Los Angeles in search of investors, Santos Bouchette shipped the necessary equipment to Catalina, and the operation was under way. His company, the Mineral Hills Mines Company, built a boardinghouse to accommodate forty employees, sank a well, and added numerous buildings to accommodate the mining camp.

The mines produced a healthy amount of galena, silver, and lead. Even gold was found, valued at between $200 to $800 a ton. Despite his new wealth, Santos was lonely. Here's where the story takes several turns.

According to one version, Santos went to the old pueblo of Los Angeles and had a passionate romance with a French dancer. They married a short time later and returned to Catalina. But a mining camp was no place for a lady, and Mrs. Bouchette soon became discontented and lonely. Santos built a fine new home for her, filling it with expensive English mahogany furnishings. But there were no mirrors, so his bride continued to be miserable. Again, Bouchette tried to please his new bride by importing a huge mirror from France. The mirror reportedly cost him $1,000.

Another Bouchette legend says that, after building a splendid home at Emerald Bay, he went to Paris to visit family . . . and to search for a bride. He met a beautiful French dancer and vowed to marry her. Returning to Catalina, he imported expensive mirrors so his beloved wouldn't be lonely. She could dance away the hours, watching herself in the huge mirrors. Still, Madame Bouchette was unhappy. Longing to resume her career as a dancer, she left her distraught husband. No one knew if she returned to France or merely danced her way to obscurity in the saloons of California.

Santos Bouchette borrowed a considerable amount of money to keep his mines operating. More than likely, his extravagance in buying expensive furnishings and clothes to please his wife gobbled up the profits. As the mines began to play out, he found himself in financial trouble. Unable to repay the investors, he left Catalina in 1876.

Even more mysterious is that Bouchette is said to have blasted the entrance to the mine closed before he left. Did he plan to return one day? Why would he bother, when there were at least forty other men who had worked there and would remember the mines' locations? It was said that he loaded a small sailboat with silver ore, quietly slipping away in the night. Had he already sent the workers back to the mainland before setting off the sticks of dynamite? If so, why did he have to sneak away?

Some accounts said his wife accompanied him to the mainland, though no record has ever been found that either of them ever arrived in Wilmington. It was also said Madame Bouchette eventually showed up in Paris. According to her friends, she and Santos landed south of Los Angeles, and her former husband had given her money to return to France. We'll never know what really happened to either of them.

When Bouchette left Catalina in 1876, he deserted his beautiful "House of Mirrors." His creditors got word he had run away. They came to the island and sold off the furnishings that hadn't been stolen by local islanders. Sadly, the exquisite mirror (or mirrors) was broken by derelicts who lived in the once magnificent mansion. In 1904, a grass fire destroyed all the buildings. Only a portion of the blacksmith shop and the stone well marked the site that had once been a booming mining camp.

MEXICAN ERA

Chapter 5

Abel Stearns: Millionaire Rancher Called Horseface

IN 1829, A BRIGHT, AMBITIOUS YOUNG AMERICAN NAMED ABEL STEARNS arrived in Old California. It was during the mission period, when Southern California was still divided into massive ranchos and Los Angeles was referred to as "The Pueblo."

Born in Massachusetts in 1798, he went to sea at the age of twelve after the death of his parents. Seventeen years later, Stearns settled in Mexico, where he became a naturalized citizen. During his stay south of the

Abel Stearns portrait (1850s).

border, he worked for a group of British merchants. This is where Stearns learned the entrepreneurial skills that would enable him to establish his own successful trading business. He must have been an affable young man, for he became friends with a number of influential, high-ranking individuals. While we don't know the details about the events leading up to the Mexican government awarding the Yankee-turned-citizen of Mexico a large chunk of land in sparsely populated "Alta California," Abel Stearns jumped at the opportunity to move to the Pueblo of Los Angeles to claim his acreage. He packed his bags and headed north.

When he arrived in Los Angeles around 1829, Stearns established himself as a storekeeper. Like other merchants of the time, he operated his business using a barter system, where rancheros and trappers exchanged hides, tallow, and furs in exchange for food and dry goods.

Over time, the entrepreneurially inclined Stearns purchased cattle for his rancho and opened a second store and warehouse in San Pedro. The small warehouse was apparently used for exchanging goods, like cattle hides and tallow (animal fat used in candle and soap making and cooking), for products from Europe or the eastern United States. Stearns apparently did business with illegal traders, as well as those who were legitimate and paid import taxes. All of this led to Stearns amassing a fortune, much of which was used to purchase as much land as he could get his hands on.

At the same time, he formed close ties with Southern California's elite—the Mexican rancheros and their families. Although he was highly respected for his great success, Stearns was a homely man with an exaggerated, long jaw. To make matters worse, in 1835 a disgruntled, drunken sailor stabbed Stearns in the face and shoulders several times in a dispute over the price of a cask of brandy. Although he survived the attack, the wounds to his face left terrible, disfiguring scars. One of the deep cuts likely severed nerves, and for the rest of his life, he had a speech impediment. Behind his back, he was called "Cara de Caballo," or "horseface."

Despite his outward appearance, it didn't slow down his business aggression. Some believed it made him stronger and even more determined to succeed. In 1840 when his San Pedro warehouse was raided by Mexican authorities, they discovered it was filled with contraband procured from smugglers. Although he was tried and found guilty, Don Abel wielded so much power in Southern California that he never paid for his crimes. Instead, in an odd and rather ironic turn of events, he was given an appointment as the administrator of customs. Two Mexican Californian governors had ordered him to leave California, and on both occasions, the governors were removed from the territory, while Stearns was allowed to stay.

When Stearns was forty-three, he decided he needed a wife. For years, he had been a close friend of Juan Bandini, one of the most prominent, politically influential ranchero owners of the Mexican period. According to Richard Henry Dana's book *Two Years before the Mast*, Bandini had fallen on tough economic times. His daughter, fourteen-year-old Arcadia, was reportedly the prettiest girl in Alta California. Stearns decided he wanted to marry the lovely and very young señorita. He was embarrassed by their age differences and wrote to the local priest asking for discretion when performing the nuptials. Then Stearns asked Don Juan Bandini for the girl's hand in marriage. Most likely, the arrangement was made without Arcadia's knowledge. When her father gave his permission, Stearns filed a petition for marriage and was granted a license in April 1841. For Stearns, becoming a member of the Bandini family was something like marrying into local royalty. With his wife's name came even more respectability from the Mexican community. In return, now one of the richest men in Southern California, Stearns helped Juan Bandini with his money problems on numerous occasions.

It's not hard to imagine the young bride's thoughts as she knelt beside her groom in the little church, Our Lady of the Angels, in downtown Los Angeles. Marrying a man nearly thirty years her senior, the man who had been given the terrible nickname of "Horseface," must have been difficult for the young beauty. But Arcadia made the best of things.

To please his bride, Don Abel built a large adobe, El Palacio, in the heart of the pueblo. The Stearns home had fine furnishings and imported décor, and it was the center of social activity in the town. With its large ballroom, the only one in the entire area, El Palacio entertained every dignitary or notable person who came to Los Angeles. Arcadia's reputation as the perfect hostess spread clear to Mexico.

By 1862, Stearns owned more than two hundred thousand acres of the choicest land in Southern California. He had scattered properties from Santa Maria to San Bernardino to San Diego and owned claims to immense grants south of the Mexican border. One of his biggest purchases in 1842 was Rancho Los Alamitos, which became the center of Stearns's vast cattle empire.

The decades Stearns had spent in California had been lucky for the Yankee merchant. That finally ended in 1862 when California's "Great Drought" began. Lasting a devastating six years, the drought caused cattle all over Southern California to die by the thousands. The ranchos suffered terrible financial losses. Dead and dying animals littered the hillsides, and there was nothing that could be done. The need for beef in Northern California in the 1850s had been a financial boom for the cattle barons of Southern California. That had already changed when ranches in the northern half of the state began raising their own sturdier stock. Closer to the markets in the goldfields, closer to the burgeoning populations in San Francisco and the other towns that had popped up by the dozens, fewer cattle drives were made to feed the northern population. The drought was the final nail in the proverbial coffin for the ranchos … including the previously untouchable Abel Stearns. For the first time, the tycoon who once made loans to help the Angelenos—who had lost money in bad investments and declining prices for cattle—was now unable to pay his own property taxes.

One by one, Stearns sold his ranchos and other pieces of property at pennies on the dollar. His pride and joy, Rancho Los Alamitos (now in Long Beach), and the Arcadia Block he had built in downtown Los Angeles went on the auction block at pitifully low prices. Finally, he hooked up with an investment company and subdivided his ranchos. Cities like Los Alamitos, Anaheim, Fullerton, Arcadia (named for Mrs. Stearns), Santa Ana, and La Habra, to name just a few, were founded on property that once belonged to Abel Stearns.

For many people, losing one's fortune that had been amassed over a long time period would have been the end of their dreams. Yet, Don Abel recovered from his financial woes and made a second fortune. His victory was short-lived, however, when he suddenly died at the age of seventy-two on a business trip to San Francisco in 1871.

Three years later, Arcadia married another wealthy American, Colonel Robert Baker, cofounder of Santa Monica. Tearing down Stearns's El Palacio in Los Angeles, which had been inherited by Arcadia, he developed the property into a commercial area, calling it the "Baker Block." Robert and Arcadia lived on Ocean Avenue in Santa Monica. Upon her death at the age of eighty-five, Arcadia was reportedly one of the richest women in America. Arcadia Bandini Stearns Baker was best known for her philanthropic work. In 1985, a bronze bust of her was unveiled in Santa Monica's Palisades Park to officially recognize Arcadia's many contributions to the city.

Today, there aren't any cities named after Stearns, and no busts of the Yankee Don can be found anywhere. Once the most successful of California's early Anglo immigrants, Abel Stearns has been all but forgotten. Abel Stearns, Arcadia Stearns Baker, and Colonel Baker are all buried at Calvary Cemetery in East Los Angeles.

Chapter 6

The Lone Woman of San Nicolas Island

CENTURIES BEFORE THE FIRST "WHITE MEN" SETTLED CALIFORNIA, THE island later known as San Nicolas was home to a group of Native Americans known as the Nicoleña. No one knows when or why the tribe decided to settle on this remote speck of an island. San Nicolas is not only desolate but also the farthest Channel Island from the coast of California. The nearest point on the mainland is about sixty miles away, and the Native people had to make the perilous journey in their small canoes.

Tiny San Nicolas is a mere nine miles in length and four miles at its widest point. About two-thirds of the interior is covered with sand, and the rest with scrub oak and coarse grass. And yet, archaeological evidence shows the island once supported a thriving Native community.

By the early 1800s, most of California's Indigenous people had been taken from their villages to one of the missions to be "civilized and baptized." While the padres at Mission Santa Barbara were aware of the tribe still living on San Nicolas, it was too much trouble to travel to the island. But when word reached the good fathers at the mission that Russian seal and otter hunters had raided the Natives' homes, killed most of the men, and stolen many of the women, they made the decision to bring what was left of the tribe to live at the Mission Santa Barbara.

In 1835, a Spanish ship headed to San Nicolas Island to pick up the surviving Nicoleña Indians. By the time the rescue ship reached the island, the sky had turned slate gray, and the wind had become ferocious. A storm front was quickly approaching. The captain realized transferring the remaining Indigenous people and their belongings to the ship in the high surf would be no easy task, and that the operation would have to be done rapidly.

The fine sand blew in a blinding shroud, making it difficult for the crew to find the Indian camp. There was a great deal of chaos when rounding up what remained of the tribe. We can only imagine the fear the Nicoleños experienced when the ship arrived. After all, it hadn't been that long since the Russian hunters had decimated their people. They were being forced to leave their homes, their island, and their centuries-old culture behind.

Here's where the facts of the story have become blurred. The traditional story is that a young woman—who was later named Juana Maria by the padres—asked her friend to carry her baby, as she was loaded down with baskets of her belongings. According to at least one version of the legend, Juana Maria was already in the skiff on her way to the waiting ship when she learned that, in the confusion, her baby had accidentally been left behind. The frantic mother tried to persuade the oarsman to return to shore. Naturally, he didn't understand her language. Even if he had, it's unlikely he would have turned back, for by now, the huge waves rolling to shore were well over ten feet high.

Desperate to save her child, Juana Maria jumped from the boat and managed to get back to shore. By now, the storm was in full force, and the ship rolled and pitched dangerously close to the reef. Fearing the ship would be lost and the crew either drowned or marooned on the island, the captain had no choice but to hoist the sails and make a run for the mainland. Eighteen years passed before anyone attempted to save the poor woman. George Nidever, captain of an otter-hunting schooner, finally came to Juana Maria's rescue. When George and his crew found her, she was wearing a robe made of animal skin covered with feathers and the wings of seabirds. The captain, who called her the "Lone Woman of San Nicolas," said she looked more like a bird than a human being.

According to Nidever, he later learned (through a translator) that, on the day the ship left without her, Juana Maria ran back to fetch her baby from the village. What she found was horrifying. The infant had been dragged off by wild dogs. Only the bloody garments remained. We can only imagine her anguish and pain. Her husband had been killed by the

Russians, and now her baby was dead, and her friends and family were gone. She was completely, utterly alone. Each day, Juana Maria returned to the beach and waited for a ship. But no one came. Somehow, the brave woman had managed to survive.

Other versions of the legend relate that her son was a teenager and that they chose to remain on the island. Historians have questioned whether or not the Lone Woman was ever truly alone. Some scholars believe that not all of the tribe agreed to board the ship that fateful day eighteen years earlier. Yet, Juana Maria was alone when she was "rescued" by George Nidever.

But the account that Nidever left us was that he was so touched by Juana Maria's plight, he and his wife took her into their home in Santa Barbara. The padres found an elderly Nicoleña Indian at Santa Ynez Mission who could communicate with her. The captain wrote that Juana Maria was fascinated by the town that had been built, by the oxen carts, and by the local people, who seemed as curious about her as she was about them. Sadly, civilization quickly took its toll on the Lone Woman. Within two months, she was dead. On San Nicolas Island, Juana Maria had survived the freezing cold winters, fought off wild animals, learned to hunt, built her own shelter, and overcame loneliness. It's believed the abrupt change of diet, culture shock, and perhaps her exposure to foreign diseases were just too much for her body or psyche to tolerate.

Juana Maria was buried at Santa Barbara Mission in Captain Nidever's family plot. Her belongings, including the feather robe, were sent to the pope where they were housed at the Vatican Museum. Her story inspired the famous young adult novel *Island of the Blue Dolphins*, written by California author Scott O'Dell in 1960.

The U.S. Navy now uses San Nicolas Island to test weapons. A heavily armed military force patrols San Nicolas, keeping curious boaters out of the area.

Author's note: Although there are several versions of this story, this account came from Frank Nidever, son of George Nidever, who remembered the days when the Lone Woman lived with his family and told and retold his father's reminiscences.

Chapter 7

Lola Montez: Spider Dancer and Countess

VISIT THE GOLD RUSH TOWN OF GRASS VALLEY IN THE SIERRA NEVADA Mountains, and you'll see the historic home of Lola Montez. During her lifetime (1821–1861), she was regarded as one of the world's most beautiful women. Lola was famous, best known for performing her sensual "spider dance" for audiences in Europe, the British Isles, Australia, and America. Why, then, did this legendary woman wind up living in a small mining town in 1853?

Born in Limerick, Ireland, Lola was originally named Eliza Rosanna Gilbert. Her father, Edward Gilbert, was in the British military and was stationed in Ireland. Edward Gilbert received orders to move to India

Portrait of the famous femme fatale Lola Montez (1847).

when Eliza was still quite young. Sadly, her father died of cholera soon after they arrived, leaving little Eliza and her nineteen-year-old mother alone in this strange, exotic country. With few choices available to a young mother and child so far from home, Eliza's mother married Patrick Craigie, another British soldier, the following year.

Eliza was an adorable child with dark curls, expressive brown eyes, and long, thick lashes. Perhaps she wasn't disciplined, or maybe she received too much adoration by the adults in her life. Whatever the reason, Eliza was out of control. She had developed a quick temper and didn't obey her parents. The problem became so bad that her mother and stepfather sent her to live with Craigie's father in Scotland. But Eliza's antics were more than the senior Craigie could take. For example, authorities caught the headstrong ten-year-old running naked through the streets of Montrose, near his home in Scotland.

As a result, her parents decided it was time to send her to an upscale boarding school in England. That didn't last long, and for the next years, she attended one school after another. Her temper and unruly behavior continued to be her nemesis wherever she went. Most likely, the pretty girl, now a teenager, believed she didn't have to follow the rules. Her effect on men may have been a way she could manipulate them. She met and charmed an older man, Lieutenant Thomas James, when she was only sixteen. Finished with school, Eliza eloped with the handsome military man around 1837.

Like Eliza's father, Lieutenant James was sent to serve in India. And for the following five years, she played the role of a married woman. But apparently, she wasn't content. There were rumors her husband abused her. Or perhaps she had merely grown bored with her life ... or with him. In any case, she wound up completely on her own and needed to make enough money to live on and to eventually return to England.

Of course, women had few choices when it came to earning a living. Eliza was determined she wouldn't marry a man simply for security like her mother had. She loved music and dancing. Her looks, she had often been told, were smoldering and exotic, all of which gave her the idea of pretending she was Spanish. She had seen the Spanish Flamenco and other traditional dances performed while living in England. That was it!

She would change her name, pretend she was Spanish, and imitate some of their enchanting dances. Eliza Gilbert re-created herself, becoming Lola Montez. A new look, a new name, and soon, a stage career. And with that, her life truly began.

Lola Montez performed in India, earning enough money to return to Great Britain. At first, she appeared in small theaters around England. Her made-up dances, she told everyone, were inspired by her country of origin . . . Spain. Her performances were so creative, so unusual, she became an overnight sensation. Her repertoire included a special routine she devised, calling it the Tarantella, or the spider dance. She wore a scanty costume that left little to the imagination and had toy spiders attached to it. She wiggled and gyrated as if to brush the spiders off in what several newspapers called "a very scandalous manner." Women were curious and men were often captivated by the beautiful enchantress. And her popularity grew.

Lola must have been fairly good, for she was eventually booked on a tour in larger, more prestigious theaters. Her appearance in London, however, was a disaster. The advertisements billed her as "Mrs. James," a divorcée who left her military husband in India. The fact that she wasn't really Spanish was also revealed by the press.

Humiliated, Lola fled to Paris. The French loved her. Europeans loved her. She performed all over the Continent, racking up numerous romantic affairs in the process. When she fell in love with the famed composer Franz Liszt, Lola spent a great deal of time with him in his later years. Through Liszt, she was accepted into the city's literary circles, becoming a close friend of George Sand, the celebrated woman author who dressed in male attire.

While performing in Bavaria for King Ludwig I, her life was forever changed. After she danced for him, so the story goes, the king asked her if her breasts were real. With her teasing smile, she pulled open her upper garment and showed him they were indeed her own. Lola became his courtesan, and their affair lasted nearly two tumultuous years. In fact, their relationship caused a near uprising among the Bavarian people, who didn't approve of the woman who had stolen their king's heart.

In 1847, Ludwig gave Lola a royal title, the Countess of Landsfeld, a royal position providing the entertainer with a generous annuity. The king was a married man with numerous children, and his queen was surely aware he had fallen in love with the dancer. But it had become more than romantic trysts between Lola and the king. The dancer had become his confidante. Lola was outspoken and often lost her temper. She had become a threat to the Bavarian people, their religion, and their politicians. She was anti-Catholic, hated the Jesuit priests, and was vocal about her belief in free thinking. Lola had already become a liability to the Bavarian hierarchy. When the king announced that he intended to make her a naturalized citizen of Bavaria, it was the final straw. The people rebelled.

Lola's interference in Ludwig's political life literally contributed to, if not caused, a revolution that ended with the king's abdication. Fearing for her life, she escaped to Switzerland, hoping Ludwig would join her there. But he never came ... which isn't a surprise when one considers he would have had to leave everything in Bavaria: his family, title (even though it was sullied), and his money. He continued to influence his country's policies through his heir, Ludwig II, builder of the fabulous Neuschwanstein Castle. Ludwig I lived the rest of his life in luxury, dying in the lovely seaside town of Nice, France, in 1868.

There was no life of luxury for Lola Montez, though she did have plenty of money from the annual annuities provided by King Ludwig I. After returning to England in late 1848, she met another military man, George Heald. The problem was that her divorce agreement with Thomas James specified neither of them could remarry while the other was still alive. When the scandal erupted, the newlyweds had to leave England so Lola could avoid bigamy charges. They escaped to France and then moved to Spain, but their marriage ended abruptly two years later when George drowned in a tragic accident. Broken hearted, Lola had to find a way to support herself. It was time to revive her stage career.

Her reputation was in tatters both in the United Kingdom and much of Europe. Yet Lola Montez always seemed to come up with a plan for her next venture. In 1851, she decided to head to America for a fresh start. Although her affair with the king was scandalous overseas, Lola used her status as a countess to her advantage. The New York City newspapers loved her, writing about her every move. It was the publicity she needed to get back on stage.

Indeed, the Bavarian countess was welcomed in the United States. Audiences were eager to see the famous beauty who caused a king to lose his crown in Europe. Not only did she perform her famous spider dance, but Lola starred in several plays, including one based on her life as consort to King Ludwig I.

Following subsequent triumphant conquests of New York, New Orleans, and other big American cities, the actress arrived in San Francisco in 1853. By then, San Francisco had already become home to wealthy men, who had either struck it rich in the goldfields, or who had sold merchandise to miners at greatly inflated prices, a practice called "mining the miners." Their mansions dotted the hillsides, and their nouveau-riche wives had become social snobs even though most had come from humble beginnings.

San Francisco was rapidly changing from a frontier town to what many called the "London of the West." The reality, of course, was that there were still plenty of bar brawls, murders, and bordellos. San Franciscans of means likely came to see Lola more out of curiosity than having high expectations of seeing a polished professional entertainer. And at first, Lola Montez filled the theater seats to capacity. Over the ensuing weeks, however, she became something of a laughingstock. The situation became so bad that a satirical play was written about the countess, mocking her singing and dancing abilities. The actress who portrayed Lola even performed a silly version of the "Spy-Dear" dance, causing a riotous reaction by the audience.

Never one to be alone for long, Lola married a local reporter named Patrick Hull in 1853. She left San Francisco with her new husband to tour some of the larger mining camps, where she was enthusiastically welcomed by grateful men who were desperate for entertainment of any kind. After her tour, she was exhausted and needed a break. That's when she set down roots in Grass Valley. She and her handsome new husband, Patrick, owned a home near the center of town. But the marriage was already in trouble. Was it her troublesome temper tantrums that broke them up so soon after their marriage?

Whatever the reason, San Francisco's newspapers announced the couple's divorce a few months later. After Hull left, Lola continued to stay in the quaint town for two more years, and the people of Grass Valley welcomed her as one of their own. She continued to make frequent trips into the mining camps to dance for her biggest fans. Trying to forget the scorn she had faced in San Francisco, she held dancing classes for the town's children. One of her students was Lotta Crabtree,[1] who would grow up to be an entertainer not unlike her mentor, Lola Montez.

Lola was fond of animals and had a good-sized menagerie on her property. Things went wrong one day, however, when she was feeding her pet bear. The animal bit her on the neck, and thankfully, the wound wasn't serious. The townsfolk held a mock trial for the bear. The "jury" acquitted the animal of the injury he had inflicted on Lola. Perhaps she wasn't amused, for she soon decided it was time to leave Grass Valley.

For the next few years, Lola wandered. She spent time performing in Australia, then returned to San Francisco for a while. She finally moved to New York City where she hoped to get back on stage. But the woman who was noted for her beauty had begun to age. So had her on-stage repertoire. It was time to change course and reinvent herself . . . again.

Still using the stage name Lola Montez, she gave lectures on the one thing she knew little about: moral issues. Rev. Charles Chauncey Burr wrote her speeches, but most likely, she provided the information she wanted to convey—cautionary tales of her life to share with young women to prevent them from making the same mistakes she had made.

---

1. Lotta Crabtree always held a special place in her heart for her mentor, Lola Montez. It had been Lola's idea to put Lotta on the stage, knowing that the girl had talent. But Lotta's mother, Mary Ann, was what we now call a "stage mother." Taking Lola Montez's idea, she cashed in on her daughter's singing and dancing. Leaving Grass Valley, Lotta and her mother traveled around the mining camps where Little Lotta performed wherever there was a paying audience. The girl's charm and adorable giggles won over the rugged miners everywhere she went. In Rabbit Creek (now La Porte), for instance, the men were so taken by her that they threw gold nuggets or bags of gold dust onto the stage at the end of each performance. In another town, legend has it that her tiny dance slippers were filled with gold.

As Lotta grew into a woman, she continued to entertain people all over America and England. By then, her repertoire had grown to include acting, playing the banjo, and singing popular Minstrel songs. When she died in 1924 at the age of seventy-seven, her worth was reportedly more than $4 million. Lotta never married, thanks in part to her overprotective mother. With no children, she donated her entire fortune to various charities.

Now in her late thirties, she gave lectures supporting women and the issues they faced.

In 1858, Lola Montez became an author, penning a small book titled *The Arts of Beauty or Secrets of a Lady's Toilet, with Hints to Gentlemen on the Art of Fascinating*. Setting herself up as a beauty expert, she wrote tips about how women could keep their skin as white and soft as possible. In France, she said, ladies took frequent milk baths, a habit all women who wanted to remain attractive should do each week. She covered topics like the proper shape of eyebrows; keeping one's hair appealing to attract men's favors; and the "beauty of the voice," which should be kept in gentle tones. She also cautioned about wearing plunging necklines, thus exposing too much of a lady's breasts. Those two "rounded mounds" should be covered and left to a man's imagination, she wrote. Had she forgotten that she exposed her two rounded mounds to King Ludwig I to gain his favor? Or maybe she had learned a lesson about using her breasts to gain the wrong kind of attention from men, and she felt she should pass along a warning to other women.

The end portion of her little book seems to be a lighthearted manual of fifty rules that men should follow when courting a lady. The jokes were more likely meant to amuse her women readers than to educate men in ways to woo the female gender.

During that time, no one knew how ill she really was. Lola was suffering from a severe case of syphilis. Just how long she had it was never known, but she had so many lovers during her short life that it's probable she had had the venereal disease for quite some time. We do know she spent her final days trying to help women in need.

After suffering a severe stroke caused by her syphilis, she died at the age of thirty-nine and was buried at Green-Wood Cemetery in Brooklyn. The name on her headstone is "Eliza Gilbert." Since her death in 1861, countless books, plays, movies, and even songs have been written about this fascinating woman. She lived her life exactly the way she wanted to—by not conforming to anyone else's expectations but her own. She rolled her own cigarettes, danced without any undergarments to shock her audiences, and loved and left men in her glamorous wake.

Chapter 8

Where the Antelope Once Played

IN 1844, JOHN CHARLES FREMONT LED A SCOUTING AND MAPPING EXPE-
dition through the *llano grande del antilope* (the great plain of the antelope), or the Antelope Valley, which is about sixty-five miles north of
Los Angeles. Members of the party chronicled accounts of thousands of
antelope grazing among the sweep of wild grasses. Little did Fremont and
his men realize that, within forty years, the antelope would be wiped out.

The first American settlers to inhabit Antelope Valley had a respect
for the small, deerlike creatures, hunting them for food when needed, and
often keeping them as pets for their children.

Unfortunately, it didn't take long for word to spread about the abundant game in the Antelope Valley. The area became overrun with professional hunters, who had been hired by Los Angeles restaurant owners
to provide "antelope steaks" for their gourmet menus. For decades, this
bloody practice continued without any regulation, until the herds of antelopes had dwindled to dangerously low numbers.

The final blow came when a group of hunting enthusiasts hired a
guide to bring them to the desert plain, where they could bag a few antelopes. Consisting of lawyers, businessmen, judges, and other professional
men, the so-called "Sporting Party," as they called themselves, couldn't
be bothered with leaving the comfortable, well-equipped camp to hunt
the animals. Instead, they waited for the paid horsemen and their pack
of dogs to round up the antelope and chase them into shooting range of
the encampment.

What was left of the antelope herds now inhabited the west end of the valley, a short distance away. It wasn't long before a cloud of dust and the sound of pounding hooves grew closer. The frightened pack of antelope was driven straight into the line of fire. What happened next has remained a controversy. In what can be called nothing less than a slaughter, the "sportsmen" unloaded round after round into the group of terrified animals. The dead and dying antelope were two and three layers deep. What the hundreds of bullets didn't do, the vicious dogs finished. Hours later, it was over. The last of the antelopes was dead. Their carcasses lay where they fell, while the hunters popped open bottles of champagne to celebrate their great victory.

Sadly, the only remnant of the great antelope herds is the name, Antelope Valley.

Chapter 9

Samuel Brannan: California's First Millionaire

SOME CALLED HIM A SCOUNDREL, A THIEF, AND A SWINDLER. OTHERS knew Sam Brannan as one of California's first millionaires, a young Irishman whose ambitions gained him wealth and status during the gold rush era and beyond. His life was filled with tragedies, disappointments, and failures. And yet, his accomplishments were awe inspiring. At the height of his career, Brannan built a railroad, founded cities, established San Francisco's first newspaper, owned an international shipping company, tried to oust the king of Hawaii and take over the islands, purchased vast amounts of land and buildings . . . and much more.

Samuel Brannan's portrait (1870s).

Nothing stopped this unusual man from achieving wealth and status. No matter what happened, no matter how much money and integrity he had lost, he rebounded with new ideas for making another fortune. He was deceitful, pious at times, and completely without scruples at other times, especially when it came to making his millions.

Why, then, did this unique and controversial man die a pauper? Even more puzzling is that, today, very few people have ever heard of him.

Born in 1819, Sam Brannan left his home in Maine at the age of fourteen to escape his abusive Irish father; he then went to live with his older sister and her husband in Ohio. A few years later, his father died, bequeathing Sam a substantial sum of money. He was a bright young man; and yet, he was sucked into a get-rich-quick land scheme that turned out to be a fraudulent investment hoax. Together with many other Ohioans, Sam Brannan lost everything.

Sam Brannan's lifelong dream had been to own a newspaper. When he lived in Ohio, he had learned the newspaper business, apprenticing at a printer's shop. After losing his inheritance, he pooled his resources with his brother, Thomas, and the two bought a printing press with the idea of starting their own newspaper business in New Orleans. That venture ended abruptly when Thomas died of yellow fever, a common disease in the swampy, mosquito-ridden city on the Gulf Coast.

Never one to give up, Sam moved from state to state, trying each time to establish a newspaper. And each time, his aspirations were crushed. After his third business failure, the discouraged Brannan returned to his sister's home in Ohio, a move that would change his life forever.

Church of Jesus Christ of Latter-day Saints

While living with his sister and her family years earlier, Brannan met several Mormon missionaries, representatives of Joseph Smith's newly established Church of Jesus Christ of Latter-day Saints (LDS). His sister and her family had joined the church, and at their urging, Sam decided to become a member. After all, he admitted that, after Thomas's death, he had been living an immoral life filled with women, liquor, and all sorts of vices. Becoming a Mormon gave him a new lease on life, and he described his baptism as "getting a fresh start."

In the following years, Brannan was enmeshed in the religion. He became a close friend of the church's founder, Joseph Smith, living with "the Prophet's" family for several years. And as a devout follower, he married a Mormon girl named Harriet Hatch in a ceremony conducted by Joseph Smith inside the Mormon Temple at Kirtland, Ohio. But the marriage wasn't a happy one, and when Joseph Smith asked him to leave town to serve a mission to proselytize the Mormon religion, Sam jumped at the chance to go, leaving his pregnant wife behind.

That's when Sam met Ann Eliza Corwin and fell madly in love with her. And yes, he was still married to Harriet, who had already given birth to his first child. But Joseph Smith encouraged plural marriage, so Sam felt justified taking a second wife. He completely abandoned his first wife and baby daughter, leaving Harriet's father to support them. Yet, Sam Brannan never looked back.

Joseph Smith asked Sam to move to New York City to start publishing a newspaper for the church. Smith realized having a church newspaper would give the LDS religion more visibility in New York, which was a perfect place to convert newly arrived immigrants to the fledgling faith.

Sam eventually wrote to Harriet, offering her a divorce. And yet, he didn't tell her he had already remarried. Reportedly, Harriet never responded to his letter, but then, he had requested his new address and location be kept secret. He wanted nothing more to do with her or his child, and he didn't want his first wife to ever be able to find him.

Despite this disagreeable situation, Sam and Ann found happiness living in New York City. Ann was expecting their first child, and Sam was the highest-ranking representative of the LDS Church in the entire state. He had brought dozens of new members into the fold, and life was good. Everything changed in 1844 when the brothers Joseph and Hyrum Smith were killed by an angry anti-Mormon mob in Carthage, Illinois. The Mormons were no longer welcome in the "States," mainly because they refused to end the illegal practice of polygamy.

Brigham Young, who had taken over Joseph Smith's position as church president, met with Brannan and assigned him the task of guiding more than two hundred church members living on the East Coast to Mexican-owned California. There, he was told to establish a town where the "saints" could live and practice their religious beliefs without inter-ference from the U.S. government. Young would lead a large group of followers overland and join the Mormon settlers in Northern California, where the church would establish their "New Zion."

Departing from New York in 1846, Sam and his family, together with 236 other mostly Mormon passengers, set sail for the West Coast. The grueling ship voyage took six long and arduous months. Ten people, including several children, died of diseases along the way. Nonetheless, after their arrival in Yerba Buena (soon renamed San Francisco), the Mormons established a small community called "New Hope" near the confluence of the San Joaquin and Stanislaus Rivers. As time passed and Young and his followers didn't show up in San Francisco, Sam Brannan became concerned that something had gone wrong.

He and several of his men rode northeast to find out what had hap-pened. And when he located the group and learned that their leader, Brigham Young, had decided to establish his new colony near the Great Salt Lake, Brannan was understandably livid. He tried to reason with Young, explaining that more than fifty homes had already been built for the church members. The soil was fertile, and there was plenty of water for farming. Brannan and Young argued, but Young refused to change his mind.

Returning to California, Sam told his flock they were free to join Young in his new settlement in the shadow of the Wasatch Mountains. Still, the Mormon leader sent several of his men to California to fetch the LDS members and bring them to Salt Lake City. Brannan was furious with Brigham Young. Why had he suddenly changed his mind? Why had he abandoned their carefully laid out plans that the "Prophet" had made before his death? Brannan became quite vocal about his disapproval of Brigham Young and the fact he had assumed the church's leadership, which many members felt should have gone to a member of Joseph Smith's family.

The discord between Brannan and the LDS Church didn't end there. Sam Brannan was disfellowshipped, despite everything he had sacrificed for the growing religion. One of the accusations against him was that he had cheated church members out of their percentage of the gold they had mined at their claim on the American River known as "Mormon Island."

In addition, he hadn't sent the profits from the gold ore to Brigham Young in Salt Lake City. The angry Brannan denied these charges and refused to send money to Young, the man Brannan believed had usurped the Latter-day Saints' leadership.

The thriving New Hope Mormon settlement was begrudgingly abandoned, and many, though not all, of Brannan's party departed. Unhappy with the way Brigham Young was running the church, Samuel Brannan settled into life in San Francisco and left his faith behind.

BRANNAN'S MANY FIRSTS

One of the items Brannan brought to California was his old printing press. He still wanted to start his own newspaper. Thus, he founded San Francisco's first newspaper, the *California Star*, in 1847. That same year, he opened a mercantile store at Sutter's Fort in what would become Sacramento.

Brigham Young believed Sam Brannan had used the money collected as tithes from the California church members to fund his businesses. For years, the Mormon leader continued to hound Brannan, sending church representatives to San Francisco to demand the money. And for years, a contemptuous Brannan ignored Young's threats.

Sam Brannan had become friends with John Sutter and John Marshall. After Marshall discovered gold at Sutter's Sawmill on the American River in 1848, Sutter and Marshall went to great lengths to keep it a secret . . . at least, for a while. But when one of Sutter's workers told Brannan about the gold strike, the wily newspaperman came up with a plan to make himself fabulously rich. Brannan owned the only mercantile store located between San Francisco and Sutter's Sawmill where gold had been found. Knowing that once word about the gold strike got out, thousands of prospectors would flood into the area, he went to every mercantile store in San Francisco and bought as many picks, pans, shovels, and other pieces of equipment used in mining as he could find. Once his store at Sutter's Fort was filled with supplies, he was ready to announce news of the gold strike to the world. First, he published a story about the discovery in his newspaper. The headline was "Gold! Gold on the American River!" Next, he shipped copies of the article to newspapers all over the East Coast. And just as he expected, the news spread around the world. Sam Brannan was sitting pretty. All he had to do was wait for the onslaught of "Argonauts" to arrive.

True to his predictions, and much to Sutter's displeasure, Brannan became rich by charging ridiculously high prices for the mining equipment. At one point, he reportedly made well over $1,000 a day (about $35,000 today). With his tremendous profits, Sam opened additional mercantile businesses in and around the goldfields. He was also confident San Francisco would eventually become the most important city on the West Coast, buying huge amounts of property all around the bay.

A few years later, Sam Brannan had become a well-known millionaire celebrity in Northern California. He moved in the upper echelons of society and continued increasing his wealth through his investments. As a respected businessman and local resident, Brannan served as the first president of the San Francisco Committee of Vigilance, known as much for their attempts to stop the violence and lawlessness in old San Francisco as for their penchant for hanging criminals before they had been tried in a court of law. Brannan's role as head of this unofficial organization made him popular with San Franciscans, yet it would come back to haunt him later in his life when he wanted to rejoin the Mormon Church.

With his newfound wealth, Sam Brannan was able to establish a trade business with China, Hawaii, and other far-off destinations. His fascination with Hawaii likely began on his first trip to California, when the ship he and his party traveled on made a stopover in Honolulu. The islands were beautiful, and there was a lot of available land that could be used for growing crops. Not only did Sam make numerous trips back to the islands as the years passed, but he also gobbled up as much Native Hawaiian property as he could.

By 1851, he had put together a scheme whereby he would overthrow the Hawaiian king and become governor of the islands. The coup was quite controversial, and his planned takeover was thwarted. Not only were the Hawaiian people furious with Brannan and his cohorts in the scheme, but he was also criticized harshly by the newspapers and non-Hawaiians living in the Hawaiian Islands.

Not all his ideas met with resistance, however. Brannan teamed up with several other investors to construct San Francisco's first wharf. And later, he built one of the city's most famous establishments, the first Cliff House restaurant, overlooking the Pacific Ocean. Sadly, the Cliff House is now permanently closed.

His other important achievements included founding Yuba City and planning the layout of Sacramento. He often traveled to the Napa Valley to "take the waters in the natural mineral springs." Believing tourists would enjoy the same benefits of the hot pools that had helped his health, he constructed a large resort in the upper Napa Valley, thus establishing the town of Calistoga. To make the resort more accessible, he began work on a railroad line to provide a more comfortable way to travel to the spa.

Not everyone was happy about having their beautiful valley developed. There were protests over the rail line. More than a thousand of Brannan's sheep were driven off a precipice in the dead of night by several local men. A mill Sam had purchased was claimed by a competitor named Snyder. When he and Sam Brannan argued over the legal matter, Snyder shot Brannan eight times. Although he managed to survive the barrage of bullets, Sam's health was affected negatively for the remainder of his life.

Pain from his wounds was more than Sam could bear. His medication came from a bottle of whiskey. He told his sister and close friends that he knew his drinking would eventually cause his demise. Yet it was the only way he could manage to get through the day.

As if Sam Brannan didn't have enough coals in the fire, he became quite active in politics. He campaigned for Abraham Lincoln's reelection, donating large amounts of money to keep him in office. In fact, he was the main speaker at the Republican Convention held in San Francisco and was one of five Californians who held the position of presidential elector in 1864.

By the early 1860s, Sam Brannan's name and the fact he was fabulously rich were known throughout America. Even the Mexican president was impressed with Brannan's many business successes. While the American Civil War raged on, the emperor of France, Napoleon III, decided to take advantage of America's weakened position on the world stage. He sent Austrian archduke Maximilian to become the emperor of Mexico, removing President Benito Juarez from his official position. The idea was that with so much chaos and loss of life in America from the war, it would be easy to send French and Mexican troops into America to conquer the entire country.

When Juarez's representatives approached Sam in San Francisco, he agreed to pump money into the Mexican president's war chest to help oust Maximilian and the French troops. In addition, he put together a group of American soldiers, calling them "Brannan's contingent." He supplied his troops with weapons, food, and everything else they would need in Mexico. Sam Brannan's plan worked, and Mexico chased the foreign intruders out of their country on May 5, 1867. For his help, Brannan was considered a hero south of the border, a fact that would later help him out of a financial bind.

During the eight years Sam's family lived overseas, his three children went to expensive schools and spoke more French than English. His wife, Ann, had become a social butterfly, flaunting her wealth as if she was royalty. Sam was tired of sending big amounts of money to Ann, and he was lonely for his family. It was time for them to come back to San Francisco. After all, their agreement was that Ann and the children would remain in Europe while the children were attending school.

Back in San Francisco, Ann was miserable. She was bored and had become what Sam said was a spoiled snob. She hated that Sam had become an alcoholic, and she believed he was a womanizer, a fact he would admit years later. She filed for divorce in the early 1870s, and in an unprecedented decision, the judge awarded her half of his entire fortune. Much of his wealth was in land and buildings. Since Ann insisted the settlement must be in cash, he was forced to sell much of his property at whatever price he could get. And, unfortunately, America was facing yet another economic downturn with the Panic of 1873. Because of the terrible economy during that time, Brannan's vast land holdings were worth less than half of what he had initially paid for them. Without the income he earned from rents collected from his many tenants, he lost most of his fortune.

Despite his love for California, and devastated by the loss of his wealth and status, Sam moved to Mexico with the hope of filing claims with the Mexican government to reimburse him at least some of the money he had provided the Mexican government to help overthrow Emperor Maximilian. He did, after all, play a large part in making this happen. Perhaps the Mexican leaders would show their appreciation by paying him with cash and land. In 1880 at the age of sixty-one, he was awarded $49,000 (equivalent to $1.4 million today), plus a large plot of land in Sonora.

Ever the entrepreneur, Sam Brannan was back in action. He spent the next few years trying to sell parcels of his land to settlers. There was plenty of water, and the area was perfect for farms or ranches. He advertised in newspapers all over America and Mexico, but not one single acre was sold. What Sam hadn't been told—and learned the hard way—was that the land granted to him actually belonged to the Yaqui Indians, and the tribe wasn't amenable to having homesteaders living and hunting on their ancient lands.

This was another blow for Sam Brannan. He used the money he had left to return to California. He had been suffering with ill health, and now in his late sixties, he was a broken man. Instead of returning to San Francisco, he settled in San Diego, where it was warmer than the Bay Area's foggy, damp weather. His nephew sent him enough money to pay for food and rent. Still, Sam dreamed of owning land again, and with his nephew's help, he was able to buy a few acres in Escondido, a small town inland from San Diego. Sadly, it would never happen. Samuel Brannan became sick, dying on May 14, 1889, at the age of seventy.

It's believed that before he died, he sent money to the LDS Church in Salt Lake City, likely to cleanse his conscience and to be forgiven for stealing from his brethren and the church's leadership.

Like many other men and women who had lived amazing lives in Old California, Sam Brannan died broke and alone. No one claimed his mortal remains for more than a year after his death. He was finally buried at Mount Hope Cemetery, San Diego, where the only thing marking his burial site was a single stake. The grave of the man who once played such an important role in California's history is now marked by a simple marble headstone. His son, Samuel L. Brannan Jr., rests beside his father.

Chapter 10

Ghirardelli's Chocolates

IN 1838, A YOUNG CANDY MAKER NAMED DOMENICO GHIRARDELLI LEFT his home in Italy and emigrated to South America to begin a new life. He wound up in Lima, Peru, and eventually changed his first name to Domingo, the Spanish version of Domenico, to fit in with the local population. It was there that he perfected his chocolate-making talents and tasty candy recipes.

Domingo Ghirardelli's portrait (1862).

When his American friend, James Lick (see Lick's story, chapter 21, "James Lick and the Lick Observatory"), who owned a piano store and several other shops near Ghirardelli's chocolate business, announced that he was moving to California, Lick asked Ghirardelli if he could bring six hundred pounds of chocolate with him. San Francisco was a growing town, and there were plenty of opportunities for new businesses. He would sell the chocolate to the local population and make a nice profit. Ghirardelli agreed.

In 1849 when news of California's gold discovery swept around the world, Lick wrote to Ghirardelli, convincing him that he needed to come to San Francisco immediately to take advantage of the burgeoning population and the fact that it was likely California would soon become a state.

Selling everything, Ghirardelli boarded a ship bound for San Francisco. Lick had written to him, explaining that San Francisco was still a bawdy town, complete with muddy streets, abundant saloons, and far too many rowdy citizens. Therefore, Ghirardelli decided to have his wife and children join him later, once the rough-and-tumble town had become more civilized.

But it wasn't candy making that would make the chocolatier his first fortune. People from all over the world flocked to San Francisco by the thousands. Before leaving for the Sierra Nevada Mountains to look for gold, each person had to purchase equipment, food, bedding, and the like in order to survive the travails they would face in the mining camps. But the "golden siren" called, and the prospectors were willing to pay the outrageous prices charged for the merchandise to make the journey.

As weeks turned to months, the flood of new arrivals didn't slow. Crews deserted the ships that transported the hopefuls to San Francisco Bay, and without men to sail them back to their home ports, the ships lay empty and rotting in the harbor.

Because Ghirardelli had arrived during the early years of the gold boom, he was able to set up a productive freight business to take supplies into the Mother Lode country. As time passed, the Italian immigrant moved his store from a tent into a new building. Believing that the city would continue its rapid growth, he used his profits to buy property and open numerous small businesses in the burgeoning city, as well as on the other side of the bay. His family eventually joined him, and with his newfound fortune, he built a large house in Oakland.

Despite his profitable real estate investments and his freight business, he longed to open another candy store. In 1852, Ghirardelli established a small chocolate factory and shop in the heart of the city. His second location was in Stockton. The delicious chocolate bars were gobbled up almost as fast as they could be produced. Even the miners who had failed to find a single gold nugget somehow squeezed out enough money to buy Ghirardelli chocolate bars.

Ghirardelli was the third chocolate maker in America, but he didn't have any competition on the West Coast. Baker's Chocolate, the biggest chocolatier in the East, was founded in Massachusetts in 1780. But because there wasn't any way for Baker's to get its candy bars shipped to the West Coast before it spoiled or melted, Ghirardelli remained king of the chocolate business throughout the western United States for decades.

Around 1867, there was another first for Domingo Ghirardelli. Hot chocolate was nothing new at this time. In fact, cocoa beans had been ground, mixed with water, and used to make a drink by the Aztecs and several other Meso-American cultures. Centuries later, a sweeter version was popular in South America and several countries. In Europe, the chocolate was melted and was often as thick as pudding. That's still the way it's served today in Spain and France.

At Ghirardelli's San Francisco factory in 1867, an accident occurred that would make hot chocolate a household regular in America. Numerous bags of sweetened chocolate paste that were ready to make into candy bars had been inadvertently left in a hot storeroom. Melting butterfat dripped into slippery puddles on the floor. What was left inside the sacks was a powdery substance. Rather than throwing it away, the workers found that it could be ground even finer and used in baking or stirred into hot milk to create an instant drink. As Americans learned to love hot chocolate, this accident would earn Ghirardelli millions more in profits.

Domingo Ghirardelli, now a widower, died in 1894 while visiting his hometown in Italy. His son, Domingo Ghirardelli Jr., took over the business and moved the chocolate plant to the block that now bears the family name. Business continued to boom, thanks in no small part to the company's accidental discovery of powdered chocolate mix.

Miraculously, the devastating 1906 San Francisco earthquake didn't wipe out the factory, though it did slow down production. Although Mother Nature failed to topple the chocolate giant, Hershey Chocolate—a new East Coast company—would eventually shake things up in Ghirardelli's domain. With the opening of the Panama Canal in 1914, and the use of railroad cars that were refrigerated with ice, shipping chocolate to the West Coast had become possible. The competition between the two famous chocolate companies became fierce.

During World War II, Hershey contracted with the U.S. government to put a candy bar in each "D" ration meal sent to the troops overseas. By the time the war had ended, Americans (and Californians) were eating their share of Hershey's chocolate.

When Ghirardelli's business declined, the family decided to sell the company. In 1960, shipping heir William Roth bought the business and converted the factory area into San Francisco's famous Square. The buildings were placed on the National Historic Register in 1983 to protect them for future generations.

Today, the chocolate company is owned by Swiss chocolatier Lindt & Sprüngli. Besides its American headquarters in San Leandro, Ghirardelli Chocolate and Ice Cream stores are peppered throughout California. A portion of the old brick chocolate factory in San Francisco's Ghirardelli Square has been converted into Fairmont Heritage Place, a luxurious hotel located close to Fisherman's Wharf. And Ghirardelli's chocolates can be found on shelves alongside numerous chocolate brands, including Hershey's candies, all over the world. Domingo Ghirardelli's success was far greater than he could have ever imagined.

The Gold Rush and California Statehood Era

Chapter 11

Charley Parkhurst: The Woman Who Dressed in Male Attire

WE'LL NEVER KNOW EXACTLY HOW MANY WOMEN IN THE OLD WEST resorted to dressing as men in order to survive. What we do know is that there were plenty of girls who were born into situations where they had few options finding ways to support themselves. School teachers and seamstresses earned a pittance. Men functioned as doctors and nurses, though women assumed the role of midwives. On the East Coast, where the Industrial Revolution would provide women's labor forces in factories, there was work. Still, they weren't even paid a living wage. Young girls from middle- or upper-class families were groomed to marry and have children; to be feminine, sew, and perform household duties. For girls who grew up in an orphanage, however, there were few choices, and their futures were often very bleak.

Charlotte Parkhurst lost her mother and father at a very early age. Spending her childhood at a New Hampshire orphanage, she must have realized her prospects of living a happily-ever-after life were very limited. Should she try to find a husband to take care of her? She wasn't pretty, and she was poor. Why should she have to marry at all? After all, she was healthy and intelligent and had learned to take care of herself in the throes of life in the orphanage. But she was told that she had no other choice. She was expected to conform; to become a mother and a wife. And she wasn't having any of it.

At the age of twelve, Charlotte reportedly escaped her circumstances by dressing in boy's clothing. Calling herself Charley, she never looked back. In fact, she lived the rest of her life in male attire, adopting men's mannerisms, gait, and habits, like smoking, drinking, and cussing, in order to keep her secret. As a man, she would have far more opportunities to earn a good wage and enjoy the freedoms that women never had.

Charley must have been an extraordinarily strong and determined individual. Still a child, the only type of job a "little boy" could procure was working as a stable hand. As the years passed, Charley learned to drive wagons, eventually graduating to a "six-horse" team. Her skills with horses were noted by James Birch, a young stagecoach driver who left for California when the news of the gold strike spread to the East Coast in 1849. Like swarms of men hoping to become rich in the goldfields, Birch convinced Charley that there were more opportunities in California than on the East Coast.

Now in her thirties, Charley bought passage on a ship bound for Panama and crossed the Isthmus to the Pacific side, where she met John Morton, a successful businessman who owned a transportation company in the booming city of San Francisco. This connection led Charley to become one of the most famous stagecoach drivers on the West Coast. She drove her stagecoaches at breakneck speed, negotiating sharp curves with ease, thwarting would-be holdups and even shooting one of the robbers. Her routes included San Jose to Oakland and Stockton to Mariposa. She carried passengers, mail, and cargo. She even drove for Wells Fargo, the first female to do so . . . even though they had no idea of her true gender.

As Charley's fame grew, so did her bank account. Life was good, despite the fact she was kicked in the face by a horse and lost use of one of her eyes. From that day forward, she became known as "One-Eyed Charley" or "Cockeyed Charley."

As the years passed and California progressed, railroads began to crisscross the country. Goods and passengers were transported by trains, and the dusty, bumpy stagecoaches were used less and less. At about sixty years of age, Charley retired and bought a farm in Watsonville, California. Fifteen years later and in failing health, she moved to a cabin outside of town. Charley had developed tongue cancer, likely from heavy smoking through the years, and she was also suffering with painful rheumatism. In December 1879, she passed away.

A few close friends came to her home to prepare her body for burial. Shortly before her death, Charley had told them she had something important to share with them. Unfortunately, she died before she could explain her real identity and why she had chosen to live as a man. Of course, the coroner had found out Charley's shocking secret when examining her body. The coroner also reported that she had given birth. A child's dress was found in a trunk in her cabin. Had she been married at some point? And what happened to her baby?

Charley's secret became such a huge sensation; the story was picked up by newspapers all over the country. As recently as 2010, the Autry National Center in Los Angeles included Charley (Charlotte) Parkhurst's story in an exhibit about homosexual, bisexual, and transgender people's roles in the Old West.

The question remains: Was Charlotte Parkhurst a transvestite, or did she dress as a man for other reasons? We may never know the truth. What we do know is that hers was a life well lived. She was successful and well respected, and she did exactly what she wanted to do.

Chapter 12

Pegleg Smith's Gold

MOST LEGENDS HAVE SOME SORT OF ORIGIN IN FACT. AS THE DECADES pass, those facts are often lost or exaggerated into tall tales. Such was the story of Thomas L. Smith, mountain man, fur trapper, horse thief, and finally, the man who is believed to have concocted a whopping yarn that has been told and retold for nearly two hundred years. But what was fact and what was fabrication? Here's what we know about Thomas Smith from eyewitness accounts and historic records.

Smith was born in Kentucky in 1801. Likely uneducated, he had earned a reputation as an excellent hunter and trapper by the time he reached his teens. In fact, he was so good that he was hired by John Jacob Astor to work alongside the likes of Jim Bridger and Kit Carson going into the rugged and untamed wilderness to provide the East Coast population with the fur of the exotic animals found in the faraway West.

Later, he shows up in documents as a scout in New Mexico. He learned to speak several Native American languages, which made him a valuable asset when leading expeditions into Indian territory. And here is where his legend truly begins.

During America's Indian Wars of the early nineteenth century, Thomas Smith was well known as an exceptionally fierce fighter. In one especially brutal battle, his shin bone was shattered by a bullet. According to his legend, when Smith realized there was no way to save his lower limb, he took out his big hunting knife and sawed off his own leg just below the knee. Ignoring the pain, he found a tree branch and carved himself a new appendage. After that, he was known as "Pegleg" Smith.

A more believable version of the story was that Smith had been shot in the leg during a battle, and his lower leg was amputated by a surgeon. Some people said it was done on the battlefield by a Native American with medical knowledge who used a hunting knife and an "Indian keyhole saw." The truth about the event didn't seem to matter. Pegleg Smith was now larger than life. They said he could fight any man, white or Indian, and win. He could even remove his wooden appendage and use it as a weapon against his enemy. As for riding a horse, he was an accomplished equestrian and could outride anyone, despite his missing limb.

According to author and frontiersman Horace Bell, who lived in old Los Angeles during the 1850s, Smith gained even more notoriety after his amputation. Bell recalled meeting Thomas Smith on a trip into the Rocky Mountains years earlier. He wrote that Smith dressed in Native attire, had a Native American wife or two, and corralled a large number of horses that had been stolen from ranches during his frequent trips into the Southwest.

Smith showed up in records years later when he worked as a trail guide, bringing amateur hunters into the wilderness so they could play at being mountain men. One of the treks he led to northern Arizona was a complete disaster. The game they sought—especially the animals with salable pelts—had been hunted to near extinction, a sad commentary about the nation's loss of wildlife. Angry at the absence of game, the hunting party disbanded and went their own way, leaving Pegleg Smith and his partner, Maurice LeDoux, without pay.

No one could ever figure out why Smith and LeDoux decided to head to Southern California after that fiasco. The most direct route was through the desert, a trail less traveled because of the harsh conditions and heat. When a sudden sandstorm blew through and completely disoriented the pair, their fate looked grim. The seasoned trail guides were lost and dangerously low on water.

That night, they camped near what they described as three low hills in what is today known as the Anza-Borrego Desert. Smith, a restless soul who had never been able to accept defeat, climbed the highest peak to better assess their location. On the way up, he noticed the hillside was strewn with small black rocks. Curious, Smith scraped one with his knife. Much to his surprise, the pebble's interior was a soft, copper-like substance. Finding his way out of the desert was his top priority at that moment. So, he scooped up a few handfuls of the stones, filled his pockets, and continued his ascent. Smith and LeDoux finally made their way to safety, winding up in a small settlement near Los Angeles. Thinking the weighty pebbles were copper that could be melted into bullets, he was shocked when an assayer pried one open and told him that the shiny substance was gold.

It wasn't until he ran out of money years later that Pegleg Smith returned to the desert to seek out his golden hillside. Strangely, Smith couldn't find it, even though the three peaks should have been an easily recognized landmark. After several more attempts, he reportedly gave up his quest.

Many people have claimed that Pegleg concocted this story so that he could sell maps to the suckers who believed his tale of gold-laden rocks just lying on the ground waiting to be found. Surely, they had been pulled out of a mine. But then, why would they have been strewn across a hillside? It was a great mystery, and for generations of prospectors, the quest for Pegleg's gold—whether it would be found on one of the three hills or in a mine he had kept secret—had begun.

As for Thomas Smith, he finally settled down in the outskirts of Los Angeles. The old Indian fighter married not one but several women from a local tribe. (One account relates that the Indians were Piute "renegades" from the high desert.) Each of his wives had brothers or cousins or half cousins whom Pegleg organized into a band of notorious horse thieves. And if there was one thing he knew besides hunting and trapping, it was quality horse flesh. California's ranchos were known for rearing purebred horses. Because the herds roamed freely grazing on the unfenced lands, they were easy pickings for Smith and his gang.

His biggest roundup occurred in the early 1840s, when he stole between eight hundred and a thousand horses from several Southern California ranchos. Los Angeles was still a rough-and-tumble pueblo, and law enforcement was hit and miss, requiring civilian volunteers to form posses to pursue the thieves.

When word arrived in Los Angeles that the rancho owners were offering a reward for the horse thieves and the stolen horses, a posse was formed. Apparently, the posse was nothing more than a bunch of "ne'er-do-wells" who saw an opportunity to make fast money, scalp "Injuns," and get some free liquor and food from the ranchos they would visit. The day they rode out of Los Angeles, the Quick Shooters, as they called themselves, were already several sheets to the wind. Instead of filling their canteens with water, they filled them with whiskey. Stopping at each rancho that had lost horses, the men were provided with food and shelter . . . and more liquor for their canteens.

Before the Quick Shooters had even left Los Angeles, however, Pegleg and his gang were well on their way out of California. When one of the Mexican Dons criticized the head of the posse for not actually pursuing Smith and his gang, the posse's leader confidently announced that Pegleg must have known the "Quick Shooters" would be in "hot pursuit." He proclaimed the posse's reputation had frightened the renegades away; that they wouldn't likely return to Los Angeles if they knew what was good for them. Besides, the horses were long gone, and there was nothing anyone could do about it. Of course, the rancheros were furious, but there was little they could do without help from local law enforcement.

Meanwhile, Smith and his Indians pushed the horses across the Antelope Valley. The animals were only allowed to pause long enough to graze or drink water and then were herded on. The pace was grueling, churning dust that could be seen for miles. The young yearlings and older mares couldn't keep up and were abandoned. But these horses were a hearty breed; their ancestors had been brought to the New World by the first conquistadores. The strays were capable of adapting to new environments and began a life in the high desert plain. As recently as the 1950s, vast herds of wild horses, remnants of the herd stolen by Pegleg Smith, were found in the remote canyons of Southern California.

Years later, Pegleg showed up in San Francisco. Drunk, alone, and broke, he continued to spin his yarns for anyone who would listen. Since his death in 1866, Thomas "Pegleg" Smith's legend of lost gold has stirred the imaginations of countless treasure hunters.

Then around 1880, there were reports of a Native American man living near Warner Springs (San Diego County) who hiked into the Anza-Borrego Desert to collect black-covered gold pebbles. He returned to his "find" frequently, though no one realized what he was doing until he was killed in a bar brawl and authorities searched his cabin. They were shocked to find $4,000 worth of these nuggets (over $102,000 in today's dollars) hidden in his bedding.

Was the story of Pegleg Smith's gold true, or did he and his partner merely concoct it? If it was all a lie, where did the gold nuggets come from? And what happened to those found in 1880? After all, many of the nuggets had been seen by quite a few people, so why hadn't anyone else been able to locate them?

THE TREASURE IS (POSSIBLY) FOUND

Fast forward to 1965 and the story written by author and publisher Choral Pepper. In her book *Desert Lore of Southern California*, she discusses her experiences with an anonymous person who sent her two pebbles of gold when she was the editor of the respected *Desert Magazine*. In his letter, the sender claimed he had found Pegleg's treasure near a rest stop about thirty miles from the Salton Sea ten years earlier, collecting a fortune from the "burned black gold of Pegleg." Ms. Pepper had the golden stones analyzed, and they were 70 percent pure gold, 20 percent silver, and 10 percent copper.

The man, whom they called "Mr. Pegleg," stated he had collected a fortune in those blackened nuggets, but he believed it was possible the shifting desert sands could reveal more in the future. The gold nuggets were on display for visitors to view at the magazine's office, but after Choral Pepper's retirement, she writes that they disappeared.

THE HYPOTHESIS

A treasure trove of gold nuggets in the middle of nowhere? How in the world did they get there? Were they from a nearby mine? Historian Robert Buck may have found the answer. One major clue was that Pegleg's ore contained 10 percent copper, and all but one of the mines in Northern California didn't have any copper mixed into its gold deposits. The exception was the gold that came from the mine owned by the famous Peralta family. The Peralta ore contained the exact same percentages of the elements as Smith's nuggets, and there was a black crust on the Peralta nuggets caused by the oxidation of the copper content.

The Peralta gold was sent to Sonora, Mexico, by pack train, and the black encrustation was left on the stones to disguise them during the long journey overland. And the old Spanish trail that they used went through the California desert. Coincidence? Not likely.

Buck believed that one of the pack trains was attacked by Native Americans, who wanted the horses. He theorized that the bags of black nuggets were simply tossed on the ground, and the guides were killed. That coordinated with "Mr. Peg's" account of finding a Spanish silver belt buckle in the area where he located the scattered nuggets.

Mystery solved? Probably, although there are still doubters who think that the treasure remains out there . . . somewhere.

In 1947, a monument was erected to Pegleg Smith in Southern California's Anza-Borrego Desert. An enormous mound of stones is nearby with a sign asking anyone who searched for Pegleg's treasure and didn't find it to throw another stone on top of the pile.

Thomas Smith's memory is celebrated each year when the "Pegleg Smith Liars' Contest" is held at Borrego Springs to pay homage to the "Greatest Prevaricator of All."

Chapter 13

Bridget "Biddy" Mason:
Wealthy Philanthropist and Former Slave

SINCE LOS ANGELES WAS FOUNDED IN 1781, MANY OF THE RICHEST AND most prominent male figures in the old town have been praised for their contributions to its growth and development. Names like Figueroa, Baker, Pico, Alvarado, Downey, Doheny, and Stearns can be found on street signs and landmarks all over the downtown area. But there has been little mention of a courageous African American woman named Biddy Mason, who came to California as a slave in 1851 and eventually became one of the richest, most respected people in the city.

Portrait of Biddy Mason (ca. 1880)

Biddy Mason was born into slavery in Hancock County, Georgia, on August 15, 1818. While there aren't any records of her during her early years, it's believed that's when she learned to use herbal medicines and basic nursing skills. She not only took care of the other slaves on the cotton plantation but also worked as a midwife for women of all colors who were giving birth.

Biddy was purchased by Robert Smith, a Mormon, and moved to Mississippi with the Smith family. One of the fourteen slaves Smith owned, Biddy likely helped care for the Smiths' six children, as Robert's wife, Rebecca, was in ill health. Biddy continued using her nursing skills for the other slaves, as well as delivering babies for both humans and farm animals. By the time she was thirty-two years old, she had given birth to three girls.

After converting to Mormonism, Smith decided he and his family would make the trek to Salt Lake City to join the other Mormons living there. There were three hundred covered wagons traveling to Utah in the group, which included everything from farm animals to dozens of enslaved people who were forced to accompany their owners on the arduous journey. It must have been difficult for Biddy and her small daughters, who all walked behind the wagon train herding several hundred livestock.

The Smiths remained in Salt Lake City for a number of years before the church leaders sent a large contingent of Mormons, including the Smiths, to San Bernardino, California, to build a new settlement. They arrived in 1851, but Smith decided to leave for Texas only three years later. Why? It was likely because California decided to become a non-slavery state, much to the chagrin of its many residents who were originally from the Southern states and owned slaves. When Smith brought his slaves to California and took up residence, they became free men and women according to state law. He must have realized he had to get his human property to a place where their status as slaves would be reinstated. And he had to get out of California before they learned they were free as long as they remained in the state.

Although Biddy had never learned to read or write, she was an intelligent woman. She had become friends with Mrs. Rowen of San

Bernardino, an ardent abolitionist. She taught Biddy a great deal, including the fact that slavery was illegal in California. Mrs. Rowen reported Smith's intention to leave California with his slaves to Los Angeles County Sheriff Frank DeWitt. The sheriff issued a writ against Smith and placed the fourteen enslaved men, women, and children under protective custody in Los Angeles.

During the momentous court battle that ensued, District Judge Benjamin Hayer decided in favor of the slaves. The judge stated it was indeed against California state law to take freed slaves back into slave states, thereby setting a precedent that was to be felt across the whole of California. It's also interesting to note Biddy was the only slave who had agreed to testify against her former owner, Smith, at the trial. This must have taken great courage, as at that time, Biddy didn't know whether or not she would have to become his slave again.

Thus, at the age of thirty-eight this tenacious woman set about making a new life for herself and her daughters in old Los Angeles. Biddy had no money, no friends, and no family in a city full of Southern sympathizers. She immediately sought a job as a midwife and practical nurse for Doctor Griffin, one of the city's first doctors, earning about $2.50 a day. She vowed she would purchase a home for herself and her children one day, and she eventually saved enough money to fulfill this promise, purchasing two lots for $250. Today, this property is located from Spring Street to Broadway, between 3rd and 4th Streets in downtown Los Angeles.

Years later, Biddy's daughter wrote that her mother "had a splendid sense of the financial value of property and such great hopes for the future of the city that she continued to buy property and retain it until after Los Angeles began to boom in the 1880s, when she is said to have sold a forty-foot lot for $12,000." She also gave her children a forty-foot lot that later sold for $44,000.

Biddy Mason began her land speculation when Los Angeles was just a remote, fledgling city. She had a vision of the future inspiring her to invest in property, coupled with a driving ambition to obtain land and wealth. This was likely the result of being raised in the old South where land and wealth were synonymous. Robert Smith and his family probably planted the idea of the importance of land in her mind at a very young age. After all, he continually moved around the country seeking more and better land to secure his wealth. Also, land speculation was one of the few ways in which African Americans were able to make money during that time.

For any or all of these reasons, Biddy took advantage of one of the few avenues open to her. She bought and sold land. In the 1880s, when the railroad lines were finally connected to Southern California, land prices soared, and Biddy's careful investments and patience paid off.

Biddy Mason is remembered for more than becoming a woman of color who became rich from investments in land. She was a humanitarian, whose charity transcended racial lines: Mexicans, blacks, and whites benefited from her generosity. This is interesting when one considers she spent more than half of her life as a slave serving a white master. It would have been natural, perhaps, for her to resent all white people, helping only those of her own race. But that wasn't Biddy. An example of this occurred in the early 1880s when a flood devastated Los Angeles, leaving hundreds of people homeless. In her usual generous manner, Biddy rendered aid to all of the victims regardless of race. Opening a grocery account in a market at 4th and Spring Streets, she allowed these people to receive food and supplies as needed, for which she "cheerfully" paid their bills.

In addition, she helped the destitute of the Los Angeles slums by providing food and money to anyone in need. She paid back taxes for her friends, and according to one source, she was responsible for founding and operating the first day nursery for orphans and the "poor and deserted children of Los Angeles."

Biddy felt a great deal of empathy toward those who were incarcerated, frequently visiting them at the city jail. She brought the men small tokens to comfort them, praying for them before she left. For this and other acts of kindness, she was affectionately known as "Grandma Mason" throughout the region.

Today, Biddy is perhaps best remembered for establishing the African Methodist Episcopal Church in Los Angeles in 1872. The first services were held in her home on Spring Street. As its membership continued to grow, the first church building was constructed at 4th and Grand on a lot owned by Biddy Mason. She even contributed $500 to the building fund. This same building was later rented by the Board of Education as the first public school for African American children in Los Angeles.

Her home located at 331 South Spring Street became a place of "refuge" for the poor settlers who migrated to Los Angeles. Long lines of people reportedly formed in front of her home asking for help from this generous woman. This practice continued until she was too feeble and old to render her assistance any longer.

By the time of her death in 1891, this remarkable woman had amassed a fortune. She left her heirs property located all over the city valued at more than $300,000 (more than $9.5 million today).

In 1909, her grandson, Robert C. Owens, was reported to have been the "richest Negro in Los Angeles." As Delilah Beasley states in her book *The Negro Trail Blazers of California*, Biddy Mason was the "most remarkable pioneer of color coming to California."

In 1990, Bridget Biddy Mason was finally recognized for her contributions to Los Angeles history when a small memorial park located near Spring and Broadway Streets was constructed. Biddy's story, "Biddy Mason Time and Place" is displayed through artwork and a timeline on an eighty-foot wall. Included are illustrations of relevant items, like a midwife's bag, wagon wheels, an early map of Los Angeles, and Biddy's freedom papers.

Chapter 14

Juanita: The First Female Executed in California

IT WAS INDEPENDENCE DAY, 1851, A DAY TO PARTY—NOT THAT THE local miners needed an excuse to drink as much whiskey as their pouch of gold flakes could buy. Jack Craycroft's Gambling Palace was the most popular saloon in Downieville, a small town in Northern California's gold country. Jack's place had plenty of booze and the prettiest gals in the whole area, including a young, black-haired beauty named Juanita. Little did she know the events that would unfold on July 4 would culminate with her execution for murdering an American man.

Cartoonish drawing of Juanita's hanging (1893).

For quite some time, tensions had run high between the American prospectors and the Spanish-speaking miners; in particular, the Mexicans, whom they referred to as "greasers." Greasers had been a name for the Mexican men who used animal fat to literally grease the wheels of their wooden carts. Now, it was a derogatory slang term used to insult a Hispanic person.

Not only did the Mexicans outnumber these newly arrived Americans and foreigners in 1849, but they had already panned and prodded some $20 million in gold from the earth. The competition for the elusive metal was fierce, and resentment against the Hispanics continued to grow with each panful of flakes they acquired. (See the Joaquin Murieta story, chapter 22.) Like many other mining camps, relations between the two races had deteriorated in Downieville, a busy mining town established in 1849.

Like so many other stories from Old California, there are at least three versions that all came from white American men. See what you think.

By the afternoon of July 4, 1851, most of the men in Downieville were already liquored up from the Independence Day celebration. The future governor, John Weller, had given a fine speech as he stood on the platform the locals built in the center of town. The mining operations were closed for the day, so there were around two thousand people in Downieville.

After the speeches had ended, quite a few of the miners planned to continue their drinking at Jack's, one of the town's saloons. A young Mexican couple were among the people employed there. Juanita, a petite girl with a pretty face, waited on tables, and her husband (or boyfriend, depending on the source), Jose, worked behind the bar.

Fred Cannon was well known in town. He considered himself to be quite the ladies' man and liked to throw his weight around. When he arrived at Jack's saloon, he was already inebriated. Women, and attractive ones at that, were a rarity in the mining towns. Not surprising was that he made inappropriate advances to Juanita. When she pushed him away, he knocked her down. Jose came to her rescue. He and Fred Cannon argued, and their fighting came to blows. The fight was broken up, and Cannon was tossed out of the barroom.

Apparently, Cannon wasn't finished haranguing Juanita, who lived with Jose in a shanty on the edge of town. According to Juanita's statement, the drunken man came to the cabin after she got off work and pounded on the door demanding to be let inside. Jose was still working at the bar, and she was alone. Frightened at what Cannon might do to her, she refused to open the door. Angry, Cannon kicked it in. There was a struggle, though it's not known if Juanita was raped. When Jose came home and found out what had happened, he'd had enough of Fred Cannon and his unwanted and hostile attentions for Juanita.

Exactly what happened next is anyone's guess. A friend of Cannon's said he had returned to Juanita's house a second time to apologize for the way he treated her and for damaging the door.

Juanita and Jose's version seems far more plausible. They said Cannon came back to the cabin a second time to finish what he had started with Jose at Jack's. Things quickly got out of hand, and the fight between the two men escalated. Likely filled with rage at Cannon, the man who had assaulted her on at least two occasions and was beating up Jose, Juanita grabbed a knife and plunged it into Cannon's chest. He died almost immediately.

Just how the town found out about Cannon's murder isn't known, but by 9:00 a.m. the next morning, both Jose and Juanita were under arrest. The debate over Juanita's fate soon began. Some folks argued that she was young—and a woman, to boot. They couldn't hang her. On the other hand, she was a Mexican—one of them—and she had killed a white man. The circumstances weren't important. Fred Cannon was dead, and that's all that mattered. The townsfolk were already riled up when Cannon's friends put his dead body on exhibition with his shirt open to show the stab wound. The bloody display was likely the last straw for those who weren't sure about what to do with the young Mexican woman.

Two men, a doctor who had been her friend and another who was a lawyer, tried to reason with the mob. Even after the doctor had told them the young woman was several months pregnant, that they would be killing two people if she were hanged, some of the men in the crowd beat him up and told him to get out of Downieville or that he would be hanged, too. A lawyer who had pleaded for Juanita to receive a fair trial was also beaten.

At first, the plan was to hang both Juanita and Jose, but since Juanita was the murderer, Jose was spared. He was dragged away and locked inside a jail cell. Given only an hour to ready herself to be hanged, Juanita was taken to her home and told to prepare for her public execution.

The accounts of the murder and her subsequent lynching varied from newspaper to newspaper, and the event grew more sensational with each of the story's retelling. After all, the more shocking the story, the more newspapers would be sold.

Most of the news reports said she bravely climbed the scaffold to meet her fate. As she stood on the makeshift gallows, she bravely, or as some articles stated, she defiantly placed the rope around her neck. They said Juanita boldly announced, "I would do the same thing again if I were treated as I have been." And then she supposedly said, "Adios, Señors," just before she dropped. According to the *Sacramento Times & Transcript* newspaper, she had "borne herself with the utmost fortitude and composure through the fearful ordeal, meeting her fate without flinching."

As the first woman to be executed in the state, her story was picked up by newspapers across the country. It was determined Juanita wasn't given a fair trial, and that there may have been extenuating circumstances in the case. There were questions raised by a lot of people who believed she had been treated badly by the men in town because she was Mexican.

The events leading up to her hanging have been debated and reviewed for decades. What had Cannon done to her when he broke into her house? Had he beaten her and done unspeakable things to the young woman? Why had she been hanged so hastily and without an authorized trial and circuit judge? Although her untimely death set a precedent for future cases, it was too late to save the poor woman's life.

While we'll never know the truth about what happened that terrible day in Downieville, researchers have found a few details about Juanita and Jose. For instance, some accounts believe her name was Josefa Segovia Loiza, not Juanita. We know the man she lived with was Jose Maria Loiza, because he later claimed damages for his wife's lynching. It's doubtful, however, that any damages were collected.

As for other popular theories about the incident, some people believe that a drunken Fred Cannon accidentally staggered into Juanita's house through an open door; that he never kicked down the door; and that he never assaulted her. And when he returned to the couple's shack later to apologize for his behavior, Cannon was confronted by Jose, who started a fight. And they think that Juanita stabbed him because she had a bad temper and was still quite angry. As for me, this author/historian/woman, I believe that Cannon was not an innocent man who was simply at the wrong place at the wrong time.

Chapter 15

Ina Coolbrith: The Poet Laureate with a Secret Past

IN 1915, AFTER DECADES OF PUBLISHING ARTICLES AND POETRY, seventy-five-year-old Ina Coolbrith was finally recognized for her body of work when she received the honored title of Poet Laureate of California. She was the first person, either male or female, to be awarded the coveted title. Since she had been a teenager, her beautiful prose appeared in newspapers, magazines, and books all over the English-speaking world. Indeed, Ina Coolbrith was special . . . and extremely talented.

Portrait of Ina Coolbrith (1893).

And yet, Ina Coolbrith had a secret past, one that she didn't share with even her closest friends. When she was born, her name was Josephine Donna Smith. Her father, Don Carlos Smith, was the younger brother of Joseph Smith, founder of the Mormon religion. Her mother, Agnes Coolbrith, was a convert to the new religion, moving from Maine to Ohio to live with the Latter-day Saints colony that had been established in Kirtland, Ohio, where she met and married Don Carlos Smith. Agnes gave birth to three daughters, the last of which was Josephine. A few months after she was born, Don Carlos died of malaria. For many reasons, including the fact the Mormons practiced polygamy, most of the colony were driven out of Ohio and moved to Nauvoo, Illinois.

A short time after his brother's death, Joseph Smith added Agnes to his household as wife number six. Records show he married a total of thirteen women the same year he married Agnes. Still grieving for Don Carlos, she had no choice in the matter. Agnes hated the institution of polygamy, but with three children, she believed there was no way out for her. (It's likely she knew Samuel Brannan, who had close ties to Joseph Smith and his family. See Samuel Brannan's story, chapter 9.)

Joseph Smith was killed by an angry mob in 1844. Agnes and her daughters fled, heading to Missouri. There, she married William Pickett, a Mormon, who promised he would never take additional wives.

In 1851, Josephine was barely eleven when her stepfather and mother decided to move from Missouri to the new state of California. In addition to the three Smith girls, Agnes gave birth to twin sons. The Pickett family was part of a group of seventeen prairie schooners heading to California, where there was plenty of land to farm, and mining towns and camps were popping up like mushrooms in the moist mountain soil. Opportunities abounded for everyone regardless of their background or social standing. And in the Far West, no one would know the Picketts were former Mormons or that Agnes's three girls had been born to the brother of Joseph Smith . . . and that she had been one of his wives.

The trek across the unsettled territories was grueling and dangerous. For decades, thousands would make the journey along the Oregon or the Southern Emigrant Trails. Many would die along the way. Diseases, heat, lack of water, and Indian attacks took their deadly toll. But for the

Picketts, the trip was worth the risks. They simply had to leave Missouri behind to begin again. No one would know who they were. The West Coast was the perfect place to hide from one's past.

During the early 1850s, the family lived in several locations in Northern California, including Grass Valley, where William tried his hand at mining. Like so many others who had migrated to California, he wasn't successful finding the sought-after ore. And again, like thousands of disappointed "Argonauts" (a name given to the swarm of prospectors who came to find gold) William and his brood moved to San Francisco, where he hoped to find work. He was, after all, an educated man who had worked as an attorney in Missouri before relocating to California. Surely there was plenty of employment in the boom town by the bay.

The unfortunate reality was that there were more men in need of work than there were jobs. Making matters worse, the prices for virtually everything a person needed to live in or near the goldfields had been drastically inflated. For example, when most of the miners were panning out around $10 worth of gold dust on a good day, a pound of butter cost $20 (or $560 today). A single egg was worth around $3, and a pound of flour could be bought for $13 a bag. Housing costs weren't any better, making it nearly impossible to afford a roof over one's head unless it was inside a make-shift tent or crude shanty. Boardinghouses and even the smallest home in San Francisco were likely out of most people's reach.

To make matters worse, fires were an ever-present problem in a town built of wooden structures. In 1855, the Picketts' bad luck continued when their house burned to the ground. Discouraged, they bid farewell to Northern California and took a ship south to Los Angeles. It was time to start over.

Mr. and Mrs. Pickett must have been shocked when they first laid eyes upon the shabby pueblo town named *El Pueblo de Nuestra Senora la Reina de los Angeles*, meaning "The town of Lady the Queen of the Angels," by its Spanish founders in 1781. It was far from being the town of angels. What they found upon their arrival was a rugged settlement replete with dusty streets, adobe houses, and more than its share of robberies, murders, public hangings, and shootouts. When they had left San Francisco, the local residents enjoyed multiple theaters, good restaurants, and several first-rate hotels. On the other hand, there were still remnants of the early bawdy days, with plenty of gambling houses and brothels. But the city was on its way to becoming one of the most desirable places to live in the country.

And now they were in the pueblo of Los Angeles. Making the best of things, William Pickett purchased a small house on the outskirts of the rough-and-tumble town and set up his law practice not far from the Plaza.

Despite the pueblo's frequent lawlessness, the Picketts settled in. Although the children attended the one and only school, Agnes spent a great deal of time educating her children. Josephine was an avid reader, enjoying Shakespeare and the classics when she was incredibly young. By the age of sixteen, some of her beautiful verses had already been published in the "Poetry Corner" of the *Los Angeles Star* newspaper, as well as in the *California Home Journal*.

Josephine was a pretty girl, and the boys in town paid her a great deal of attention. Robert Carsley, a handsome part-time actor and iron worker, was the man who won her heart. The couple married in 1858 when she was barely seventeen, but it was a doomed union. Not only was her husband physically abusive, but Josephine gave birth to a son, who died as an infant. After suffering ill treatment at her husband's hands and in a deep depression, she moved back home with her family.

Josephine's husband wasn't having any of his wife's rejections. Upon returning from a trip to San Francisco, he found that Josephine had moved out. Enraged, apparently assuming she had left him for another man, Carsley went straight to the Picketts' house, shoved his way past Josephine's mother, and grabbed his wife. Threatening to kill her if she didn't go home with him, he dragged Josephine outside by her hair. That's when William returned home and saw Carsley abusing his stepdaughter. Yelling at the half-crazed man, Mr. Pickett took aim and fired at Carsley. He missed. When Josephine broke away and ran, Carsley drew his gun and shot at her. The bullet missed, whizzing past Josephine's mother, Agnes. Mr. Pickett took another shot when Carsley took aim again at Josephine. This time, the bullet struck the irate husband in his hand, doing so much damage it had to be amputated.

A sensational divorce trial resulted, in which William Pickett was exonerated and Robert Carsley was jailed. The entire Pickett family had testified as to Carsley's attempts to kill Josephine; all except poor Josephine, who was spared the embarrassment and upset of having to tell the sad story of her hellish marriage.

The scandal was more than the Pickett family could bear. William, Agnes, their young twin sons, and Josephine left Los Angeles and their bad memories behind and headed back to San Francisco. The other two girls stayed behind; in fact, one of them had married a Mormon man and lived in the then-Mormon community of San Bernardino.

Wanting to put the terrible marriage behind her and make a fresh start, Josephine decided to change her name. When Josephine was a schoolgirl in Los Angeles, her friends had often called her Ine or Ina. Her mother's maiden name was Coolbrith, so she began to call herself Ina Coolbrith or Donna Coolbrith. For the rest of her life, no one knew her as anything other than her new name. Ina Coolbrith became famous, and the name Josephine Smith and her past were forgotten.

She continued writing after she and her family moved back to San Francisco. In fact, as the years passed, she wrote with Bret Harte for the new *Overland Monthly*. Her literary works received great reviews in the *New York Times*. She had connections with Lord Tennyson, John Muir, and other famous people living in the Bay Area. Henry Wadsworth Longfellow praised Ina, writing that California had at least one great poet. Ina rubbed shoulders with such literary icons as Samuel Clemens (Mark Twain), a young Jack London, Robert Louis Stevenson, and Charles Fletcher Lummis.

In 1871, her dear friend and fellow writer, Joaquin Miller, asked her to care for a teenaged Native American child named Calla Shasta (Lily of Shasta) while he was away in England. Miller, whose real name was Cincinnatus Heine Miller (nicknamed "Poet of the Sierras"), had become quite famous as a frontiersman poet. He was also known for his adventures living with the Wintu Native Americans and for marrying a woman from the tribe. Ina knew Calla Shasta was Miller's daughter and agreed to care for the child. Oddly, Miller never returned to claim the girl.

As the years passed, Ina's earnings from her writing didn't bring in enough money for her to take care of her growing family. She supported her aging mother, her sister who was battling cancer, her sister's two children, and Calla Shasta. This burden meant Ina would have to find full-time employment, which would leave her little time to write. With no other choice, she moved the entire family to a large home in Oakland in 1874, accepting the position of librarian for the new public library, a job that lasted for nearly twenty years.

Her employment ended when she was abruptly replaced by her young nephew, who had little literary expertise. The wound cut deep. It became obvious her age and the fact she was a woman factored into the library director's decision to let her go.

She worked in a few other libraries for a while, but she was anxious to get back to her poetry. After years of supporting and caring for so many family members, they were finally all gone, and her life was her own again. She moved back to San Francisco, living in a small apartment. Her writing gushed out like a geyser, as if her thoughts and emotions had been pent up inside just waiting to surface after a prolonged period of dormancy. She spent time with other poets, holding Parisian-style literary salons in her home and fully enjoying her resurrected life in the arts.

Then on April 18, 1906, fate dealt Ina another terrible blow. Like thousands of San Franciscans, an earthquake shook her awake at 5:12 a.m. There was only enough time for her to grab a few things before running out of the collapsing building. The streets were filled with stunned and injured people. Buildings were on fire. Dust and smoke made visibility difficult. Though Ina survived, her belongings and her writings did not. An autobiography she had worked on for months and numerous new poems were incinerated in the fire that consumed most of the beautiful city. She lost her large library of books, photographs, and priceless memorabilia . . . everything was gone.

Disheartened, Ina Coolbrith, who had once loved San Francisco and all things California, moved to New York City to put her past behind her. Years later, when she was in her early eighties and in declining health, she returned to the Bay Area to live her remaining years with her niece in Berkeley. She brought fifty-five new poems with her, all ready to be published. They were another treasure of beautiful, flowing verses that would become part of Ina's legacy. In Northern California, the chilly weather wreaked havoc on her rheumatism. And yet, she continued to write poetry.

The story of her Mormon upbringing wasn't known publicly until her cousin, Joseph F. Smith, revealed her personal history in 1917. Ina was furious with Smith, with whom she had continued a friendship since they had been children. Ina had decided years earlier that she didn't want anyone to know her family members were polygamists. Like her mother, she despised the practice of allowing male church members to have multiple wives. But Smith had an agenda and wanted the world to know his famous cousin was more than a poet and writer. He constantly reminded her she had "royal" blood coursing through her veins . . . the blood of the founder of the Mormon Church, Joseph Smith.

Ina never had the heart to write her autobiography again. Her life had been amazing, though it was filled with too many ups and downs for one person to experience. Years earlier, she had made a commitment to her publisher to write a memoir about her acquaintances and friendships with many of the most famous writers in history. The book was never finished. Ina later wrote that, if she had published it, the contents would have been "too sensational" for suitable reading. Was the real reason she chose not to write it because she didn't want to be associated with the Latter-day Saints? She had certainly intended to keep the truth a secret. Did it make a difference in her popularity? Her writing career? Probably not, but it was a subject too personal for her to discuss.

At the age of eighty-four, Ina Coolbrith was awarded an honorary master of arts degree by Mills College, a women's college, in recognition of her massive body of works. In 1925, a program was held to honor her accomplishments. It was attended by more than five hundred children who had been raised reading her lovely poems. Author Charles Lummis, who accompanied her to the presentation, told Ina she was the most remarkable woman alive—a poet who would be remembered not only as California's greatest and beloved poet but also as a poet whose words would be read and cherished by generations of people around the world.

When she died in 1928, Ina Coolbrith was recognized as one of the most prolific poets in history. Not only was she California's first Poet Laureate—a woman who was called the "Sweet Singer of California" by literary communities all over the country—but she was the first person to be recognized as a Poet Laureate in any state. Ina, who was likely frustrated that death was interrupting her ability to continue to work, was laid to rest in Mountain View Cemetery in Oakland, California.

Today, the Library of Congress and the National Archives have hundreds of her lyrical, rhythmical works. From her depictions of everyday experiences to the death of loved ones, to her descriptions of nature that simply glide across the page, Ina Coolbrith was a master at her craft.

Chapter 16
Firebrand Lillie Hitchcock Coit

Most residents of San Francisco, as well as many visitors, are familiar with the name Lillie Coit. After all, Coit Tower, the well-known landmark atop Telegraph Hill that stands like a beacon overlooking San Francisco, was named to honor Lillie. And yet, very few people know her story. Indeed, Lillie Hitchcock Coit was far more than the local legend who was a devoted fan of the San Francisco Fire Department. She was truly a firebrand, a woman who did it all and didn't care what people thought, during a period in history when women were supposed to behave like genteel ladies.

Not considered beautiful, Lillie still mesmerized people wherever she went (1862).

Born at her parents' home near West Point Military Academy in 1843, Lillie was named Eliza Wychie Hitchcock. Because she was so fair skinned, they began to call their daughter Lillie, and the name stuck. The Hitchcock family moved to San Francisco when she was only seven. Her father was a West Point graduate and a military physician who had been assigned to the San Francisco Presidio. On the final leg of their journey to San Francisco after their trek through the jungles of Panama to get to the Pacific Ocean, the coal piles in the ship's below-deck storage bins caught fire. Shipboard coal fires were common during those times, and many steam-driven vessels were lost at sea as a tragic result. Luckily, the crew was able to snuff out the flames after several touch-and-go days, and they steamed safely into San Francisco in May 1851.

It didn't take long for the ship's passengers to learn that many of the town's wooden buildings, including the boardinghouses and hotels, had been destroyed in a recent fire. While most of the new arrivals would have to live in tents for the time being, because of Dr. Hitchcock's status as a military officer the Hitchcocks were invited to stay at the most fashionable boardinghouse left in town. Things went well until a few months later, when another fire swept through the neighborhood, burning everything in its path. The Hitchcocks lost most of their belongings when the blaze destroyed the structure. And once again, they were without a place to stay.

They were invited to live with Colonel Joseph Folsom (for whom the town of Folsom is named) for a while. Lillie was quite fond of the colonel, and he returned her affection. During that time, the Hitchcocks socialized with the ever-growing population of upper-crust men and women who continued to move to the fledgling city.

Lillie's wealthy father and mother were from the South. Both of their families owned plantations and dozens of slaves. Lillie's mother, Martha, had been so pampered growing up on a plantation that she didn't have the skills to run her own household after she was married. When the Hitchcocks finally had their own home in San Francisco, Martha sent letters to her family requesting they send her enough slaves to cook, clean, drive their carriage, and take care of headstrong little Lillie.

Although California would eventually become a "free state," a number of Southerners brought their slaves with them when they moved to

California (see Biddy Mason's story, chapter 13). Of course, that all changed after the Emancipation Proclamation of 1863 and particularly after the end of the Civil War. California had supported the Union throughout the war, much to the chagrin of the large number of Southern Democrats who tried repeatedly to make slavery legal in the Golden State.

But Martha Hitchcock had her slaves living with her before those changes occurred . . . or, at least, until there was enforcement of the anti-slavery laws. On one occasion, Jeanette, the young slave who took care of Lillie, made the mistake of taking the feisty child to a party at the military base while Dr. and Mrs. Hitchcock were away for a while. Lillie insisted she wanted to attend, and poor Jeanette gave in to the child's demands. Returning home, the parents discovered Jeanette and Lillie were gone. When Dr. Hitchcock found them at the fort barracks, he was so angry that he struck the slave girl with his cane.

Jeanette ran away from their home later that evening, and Dr. Hitchcock called the police to find her. She was located hiding at her friend's house. Both women were slaves, so the police arrested the two of them and took them to the jail. When Dr. Hitchcock arrived, he flogged each of them with thirty-nine lashes—Jeanette for trying to escape and her friend for harboring a fugitive.

It's believed both Martha and Lillie were upset by Dr. Hitchcock's wrathful behavior, but there was little they could do. Records indicate that Jeanette was sold because of her continued attempts to escape.

Despite having numerous slaves to do her bidding, Martha grew tired of running her own household. The spoiled heiress decided it would be best if the family moved to the finest hotel in San Francisco, a place where she could live in as much luxury as was available. With that, the remaining slaves were sent back to Martha Hitchcock's family plantation, and Martha, Dr. Hitchcock, and Lillie moved into a newly completed hotel.

One of the downsides to living in a fancy hotel was that there were very few children to play with. At Lillie's insistence, her mother allowed her to accompany a business friend of Dr. Hitchcock's, Mr. Fitzmaurice, and his two children, a boy aged twelve and his nine-year-old sister, to a tea party. On the way, the man decided to make a quick stop to inspect his new hotel, which was still under construction.

While Mr. Fitzmaurice busied himself looking at the building plans, Lillie and her two friends decided to go inside the half-finished structure to play. They climbed the stairs to explore the upper floors. When Mr. Fitzmaurice noticed smoke billowing from the hotel's open front door, he realized the children had gone inside. Running into the structure, he saw that a fire had ignited in the lobby. The children were nowhere to be seen. Yelling, he heard their voices coming from somewhere upstairs. By now, the staircase was completely ablaze. He shouted desperately for the children to find the back staircase. But in the melee, his two children panicked and ran down the stairs toward him. Standing her ground, Lillie screamed at them to stop. Moments later, she watched as a burning beam crashed down on her friends, burning them to death.

We can only imagine the horror that she experienced. She was surrounded by flames, and there was no way out. And then a miracle happened. A volunteer of the Knickerbocker Number Five fire company was lowered through a hole punched in the roof. He plucked the frightened girl from the flames an instant before she would have been burned alive.

The horrible experience forever changed Lillie's life. Firefighters became her heroes. Amused by her devotion to them, the men of Knickerbocker Number Five appointed the girl to be their unofficial mascot. She eventually rode with them in parades and attended celebrations with all the city's fire companies. She was so fascinated by firemen that she reportedly followed them to fires in downtown San Francisco, cheering them on as they rescued victims from burning buildings and fought to snuff out the flames.

As the years passed, Lillie became famous as the symbol of volunteer firefighters, reportedly embroidering "No. 5" on her undergarments. When she was about twenty, Lillie received an official certificate of membership in Knickerbocker Number Five, becoming the only woman in the country to belong to a fire company . . . even if it was in name only.

The spirited young woman became known throughout San Francisco for more than her love of firefighters. Lillie had inherited a great deal of money from her grandfather. Though she wasn't beautiful, she wore lovely clothes and had an infectious personality. Part of her appeal was that she was an accomplished musician, dancer, and singer. Her money enabled her to do things that most other women would not have dared during this restrictive Victorian period. For instance, Lillie was fond of "unladylike" pastimes, such as playing poker and betting on horse races, diversions generally enjoyed only by men and "lower class women." But no one seemed to mind. She was charming, likable, and extremely popular. Local papers called her the city's "brightest ornament" and the "belle of San Francisco." Men from every social status sought her hand in marriage.

Turning down more than one proposal, Lillie had set her sights on the handsome, rich Howard Coit. And what intractable Lillie wanted, she usually got. But her dreams were put on hold when her mother whisked her off to live in Paris around 1861. The Civil War had begun, and like many other wealthy Southern women, Martha and Lillie had to be shielded from the vulgarities of war—especially a war that threatened the lifestyle that Martha cherished . . . including owning slaves.

Lillie had a big personality, and she certainly didn't go unnoticed in France. In fact, she became a favorite in the court of Napoleon II. She was literally the belle of the ball wherever she went. And yet, as soon as the war ended in the United States, Lillie returned to her beau in San Francisco. She married Howard Coit in 1868. Not surprising was that the fashionable couple became a big part of San Francisco's social scene. Lillie's joyful bubble burst, however, when she discovered that her husband was having an affair.

Although the couple separated, Lillie never filed for divorce. Instead, she decided to leave the city. The Hitchcocks owned a great deal of property in what is now the wine-growing country of Napa. Martha Hitchcock had two homes built—a large one for herself, and a slightly smaller adobe house for Lillie. Things took an unexpected turn when Howard Coit died at the age of forty-seven. Hardly the grieving widow, the now middle-aged Lillie emerged wealthier, happier, and perhaps a bit feistier than ever.

Moving back to the city, she had encounters that were beyond scandalous. For example, Lillie disguised herself as a man on more than one occasion in order to experience the seedier side of San Francisco's night life. She loved to gamble, went to cockfights, and took camping trips with her male companions, all of which shocked the city's pretentious residents. Renting a suite at the elite Palace Hotel, she hired two professional boxers and (unbeknownst to the management) held a match in her suite to entertain her men friends.

When the newspapers got wind of Lillie's latest fiasco at the Palace Hotel, tongues wagged. No longer the city's sweetheart, Lillie finally became a social outcast. The spirited woman had apparently had enough of the city's gossips, for she left San Francisco and moved to Europe for several decades, where she could live life as a free spirit. Still, she never forgot San Francisco and decided to return to the City by the Bay in her old age. By then, most of those who had condemned her had passed away or had forgotten Lillie's antics.

Lillie Hitchcock Coit died at the age of eighty-five, and in her will she bequeathed the city the sum of $100,000 (more than $1,600,000 today). Remembering her admiration for San Francisco's firefighters, the city used the money to build an observation tower on Telegraph Hill, named in her honor, and constructed a monument to the city's firefighters in Washington Square. Coit Tower continues to be one of San Francisco's most famous landmarks.

A rather remarkable coincidence is that many people believe Coit Tower resembles the nozzle of a fire hose. Though the architects stated that it was never their intent, the tower's design is certainly a fitting tribute to one of San Francisco's most interesting former residents.

Chapter 17

Eleanor Dumont and Women in the Gold Rush Era

WHILE HORDES OF MEN MADE THEIR WAY TO SAN FRANCISCO DURING the early gold rush years, there were occasional female arrivals who came from a variety of countries to make their own fortunes. A few would actually prospect for gold, but most were prostitutes, a much-welcomed commodity among the lonely miners.

During the early years of the gold rush, most "decent" women refused to live in San Francisco; especially in the uncivilized mining camps in

Dumont was said to be a beauty in her younger years; her looks didn't improve with age (1860s).

the mountains. When a ship with young women passengers arrived in the port, word spread like a wildfire. Of course, not all of the miners were single men, but were husbands and fathers who had left their families behind. Occasionally, a wife traveled west with her husband, so when another group of questionable women arrived, the "upstanding ladies" in town vocalized their anger.

At that time, men outnumbered women by around one hundred to one, and even females with below-average looks were a sought-after prize. East Coast newspapers ran advertisements paid for by desperate men in the gold camps, hoping to woo a wife west and into his arms. But word had spread in the East that the goldfields were still violent places where most "decent" women weren't willing to live.

As the "unsavory" women continued to come, the hundreds of saloons and brothels that popped up throughout the region did a tremendous business. Most revered by the miners were the French ladies, who set themselves apart from the other women of questionable virtue by maintaining an aura of femininity, dressing well, and perfuming their bodies. Because of their revered reputation in the boudoir, they were more expensive than the other, less experienced prostitutes. And the gold dust kept pouring in.

A large group of these lovely mademoiselles stepped off a French ship in San Francisco in late 1849. Among them was Eleanor Dumont, a pretty young woman in her early twenties. Not all of them were prostitutes. Eleanor's ambitions were set much higher. During her heyday from the early 1850s to the 1870s, Eleanor Dumont earned the reputation as the best woman gambler in the West. She had no trouble finding work in the city's countless gambling establishments, picking up the tricks of the trade by observing the moves of professional gamblers. The dark-haired, shapely French beauty was something of a sensation in the growing town. Not only did she speak five languages, an advantage when many of the immigrant gold seekers only spoke their native language, but Eleanor was witty, knowledgeable, and an accomplished musician. She was always dressed to the nines, wearing expensive and fashionable clothes and jewels. Besides her attractiveness and charm, Eleanor's manners were impeccable, all of which made her even more appealing.

Meanwhile, the gutsy women who arrived from various countries made plenty of money in Northern California. For those ladies who were so inclined, gambling halls were extremely popular in San Francisco during its boom years of the 1850s, and female card players were a novelty. Who better to deal a hand of cards than the soft-spoken, alluring Eleanor Dumont?

"Madame Dumont" opened her own gambling house in Nevada City in 1854. She sat at her gaming table each evening sipping champagne, as a steady flow of eager men waited to lose their hearts and gold to the lovely French woman. Her specialty was high-stakes gambling, and bets of $20,000 weren't uncommon at her table. The classy lady offered her "guests" free champagne.

Before sitting down with the enchanting Madame Dumont, however, they were advised they couldn't spit tobacco on the floor, cuss, or fight—all standard practices in most saloons at that time. The grimy miners actually bathed and wore clean clothes before playing cards with her. They were beguiled by her and were happy to follow her rules.

Over the next nine years, Eleanor Dumont's fame spread through the mining camps. By 1859 when Nevada City's gold ore had been played out, she had accumulated a small fortune. When the miners, many of whom were her best customers, moved to Virginia City, Nevada, she followed. A rich deposit of silver ore had been discovered, and new fortunes were made, both by the prospectors and Eleanor Dumont.

Eleanor took her money and settled down, marrying David Tobin. Retiring to a Nevada farm with her new husband, the French woman dropped out of sight. Legend has it that the handsome Tobin was a scoundrel, marrying Eleanor for her money. As the years passed and the money dwindled, he left her broke and alone.

Devastated, she attempted to pick up her gambling career where she had left off. But by now, her shapely figure had thickened, her face was wrinkled, and a layer of black downy hair had grown across her top lip. The men began to call her "Madame Moustache," a moniker that dogged poor Eleanor the rest of her life—and well beyond the grave.

By then, women weren't as scarce as they had previously been in Northern California. The once-captivating French woman had to compete with the younger, more attractive girls who continued to flow into the mining towns from San Francisco. Likely depressed and struggling to make ends meet, she began to drink heavily.

Eleanor hadn't resorted to prostitution. But now, she had run out of options. Bitter and hardened, she finally gave up her principles, resigning herself to working in a brothel. The former sophisticated French lady learned to use a horsewhip to defend herself from the drunken miners who could often be abusive. On at least one occasion, she killed a man who tried to rob her.

Moving to the rough-and-tumble mining town of Bodie, California, in the 1870s, things continued to spiral downward. Madame Dumont gambled and drank away what little money she made. Unable to cope with what she had become, an aging, overweight alcoholic, she drank her last glass of champagne on September 8, 1879. It was laced with poison.

The *Sacramento Union* ran a short blurb, which read, "A woman named Eleanor Dumont was found dead today about a mile out of town, having committed suicide."

Madame Moustache was buried in Bodie "outside the fence," as only "decent, law-abiding folks" were allowed inside the main cemetery.

Chapter 18

California's Giant Sequoias

NATURALIST JOHN MUIR ONCE CALLED CALIFORNIA'S GIANT SEQUOIAS "nature's finest masterpiece" and "the greatest of all living things." Since their discovery more than 160 years ago, travelers from all over the world have come to California to behold the majestic trees.

Not only are the stately Sequoias among the oldest living things on the planet, but their ancestors can be traced back millions of years. Around seven million years ago, the massive groves disappeared from ranges in northern Europe and most of North America, with the exception of the western slope of the Sierra Nevada Mountain range in Central California. Apparently, it was this area that provided the perfect soil and climatic conditions needed for the trees to survive.

The first humans to set eyes upon the massive trees were Native Americans, possibly hunters who ventured into the rugged Sierra Nevada Mountains in search of game. While the name of the first white man to gaze at the towering forests is still debated among historians, one of the earliest "discoverers" was a man named A. T. Dowd.

After gold was discovered in California, tens of thousands of men flooded into canyons and gorges of the mountains in and around the Mother Lode country. As the canvas encampments evolved into towns, timber for the buildings was felled from the local forests. In the wake of the building boom, as the wooded areas close to the goldfields disappeared, wildlife retreated farther into the mountains, and food became harder to obtain.

In 1852, a company in Murphy's camp (near the Stanislaus River) hired A. T. Dowd and three other hunters to keep their loggers and carpenters fed. One day, while Dowd was on the trail of a grizzly bear, he followed the tracks deeper and deeper into the forest. Suddenly, Dowd realized he had stumbled upon what was surely one of the great wonders of the world. Before him was a forest of giant trees. He later described the titans as being wide as a house and having a crown so high that he couldn't see the tops. Stunned by what he saw, Dowd completely forgot about the bear and hightailed it back to town to share the news. Mocked and jeered at, accused of having an overactive imagination or too much whiskey, and knowing that no one would hike fifteen or twenty miles to see the mammoth trees, he changed his story. Instead of huge trees, he told his friends that he had killed the biggest grizzly bear in California, and that he needed their help hauling the carcass back to Murphy's camp. He even offered each man a juicy bear steak for their trouble.

Dowd's ruse was successful. A few hours later, he and his party reached the forest of gigantic trees. One of the men who accompanied Dowd, James M. Hutchings, wrote a book about this experience, titled *Scenes of Wonder and Curiosity in California* (1862).

News of the great trees spread around the world as quickly as the discovery of California gold had traveled in 1849. Scientists excitedly worked to categorize and study the ancient trees. A German botanist gave the trees their name, *Sequoiadendron giganteum*, or Giant Sequoia, in honor of the great Cherokee leader, Sequoyah. No one seems to know why the scientist decided to use the name of the famous leader of the Cherokee nation. After all, Sequoyah had never been to California, and there was no obvious connection. By the time of his death in 1843, the Cherokee leader was the most famous Native American in the world. The German obviously had great admiration for Sequoyah's many accomplishments and thought the most splendid trees in the world should bear his name.

Sadly, loggers didn't share the scientists' enthusiasm for the Sequoias' stately grandeur. Instead, they saw easy money. Many of the colossal forests were cut and leveled, dramatically reducing the number of trees within twenty-five years after their discovery. By the 1890s, the U.S.

government recognized that, if legislation wasn't passed to protect the Giant Sequoias, they would one day disappear. As a result, in 1890 Sequoia was named the second National Park by President Benjamin Harrison (Yellowstone was the first). Soon thereafter, Yosemite and Kings Canyon National Parks were created, as well as numerous California state parks.

The National Park Service was created to protect our national treasures in 1916, when the federal government decided to keep these beautiful areas safe from logging and development for all time. As word spread about the Giant Sequoia trees, tourists hoped to travel to Central California to experience their magnificence. The problem was that there wasn't much of a road into the park. Instead, during the early years, access was by pack mule, and Captain Charles Young, the only African American commissioned officer in the United States Army, was sent to take charge of regulating and accommodating the ever-growing number of visitors. The first road was finally completed in 1903.

Today, the seventy-five Giant Sequoia groves are scattered across a 15-mile-wide, 260-mile-long strip of land. Millions of visitors from around the globe have come to see the Giant Sequoias, the largest living things to ever inhabit the earth. The General Grant Tree in Sequoia National Park is more than three hundred feet tall and is estimated to be around 3,200 years old.

Together with its cousin, the California Redwood, the Giant Sequoias were appointed as the California state tree in 1973.

Chapter 19

California's Cotton Boom

Few people know that cotton was grown in California as early as the Spanish period. Unlike planters in the American South, the rancheros didn't use cotton as a cash crop. Instead, it was woven into fabric for clothing and various other necessities.

California's true cotton boom began shortly after California became a state. By the early 1850s, farmers who had immigrated from the South were already growing "a cotton of superior quality." But could the cotton industry produce as much revenue as cattle ranching or growing wheat? Speculators gambled fortunes hoping they would grow even richer from producing cotton. For example, Matthew Keller converted eighty acres into a cotton plantation in what is now downtown Los Angeles. Another of Keller's cotton farms was located where the University of Southern California was later built. He was quite pleased that his plants had produced abundantly, stating that the cotton bolls (not balls) had burst with so much of the fluffy white stuff that his fields looked like an "Arctic landscape."

John L. Strong, who had moved from Mississippi to Merced, transformed several hundred acres into a cotton farm. Later contracting with the Los Angeles and San Bernardino Land Company, he planted six hundred acres of cotton on one of Abel Stearns's ranchos near Santa Ana. (See the story of Abel Stearns, chapter 5.) Touting his successes, Strong published several articles claiming that his experiments had proved that California could produce a better grade of cotton than that grown in the

South. Newspapers, magazines, and government periodicals publicizing Strong's experiments believed that California would quickly become the leading cotton-producing state in the Union. Logically, it should have.

When the Civil War broke out in 1861, the North's supply of cotton from the Southern states was cut off. Naturally, that created a huge demand for the "bolls." Not only did half of the population of the United States need cotton products, but the Union army had to find fabric from which to make thousands of military uniforms. But for some strange reason, California's cotton growers didn't jump on the bandwagon and fill the void left by the absence of Confederate cotton. Instead, San Francisco's wool producers beat them to the punch, providing the Union army with woolen uniforms and blankets—which were fine for the winter months, but were scratchy and miserably hot in the summer.

Maybe Southern California's cotton growers failed to get their products to the Northern market because there was a shortage of ships during the war years. Or perhaps it was because San Francisco's wool-growing and milling industry was already up and running, quickly answering the army's demand. More than likely, though, it was because the pro-slavery former plantation owners who supported the Confederacy refused to provide their product for the Union army's military uniforms. In any case, these and other disastrous events during the 1860s dealt the state's cotton industry a hard blow.

After the Civil War ended in 1865, the California Cotton Growers and Manufacturers Association purchased ten thousand acres of land in what is now Bakersfield. The association imported a colony of experienced cotton field laborers, African Americans from the South, to plant, cultivate, and gin the crop. These newly freed slaves soon discovered they could earn more money doing jobs that paid better and didn't demand the kind of backbreaking labor they had experienced in the cotton fields. When the entire workforce deserted, the cotton crop went to weed, and the growers were bankrupted.

Despite these failed beginnings, cotton would soon become a part of the state's agricultural family. By the early 1880s, California Cotton Mills, which employed some seven hundred workers, was founded. The company used cotton grown in the Imperial Valley to manufacture a large variety of goods, like canvas, comforters, and tablecloths, which were shipped all over the nation. The San Joaquin Valley was also a prime place for cotton farms.

By the 1930s, Mexicans and Mexican Americans made up more than 70 percent of the cotton field workers. The balance of the Depression-era laborers were Dust Bowl migrants from either Oklahoma or Arkansas.

Today, California's cotton industry has slipped to tenth place in annual production in the United States, due in part to the recent droughts. To stay afloat, former cotton farmers have had to switch to more lucrative crops like growing almonds. It's a sad ending to one of the Golden State's great success stories.

Chapter 20

Chinese Squid Fishermen and the Exclusion Act

THE CHINESE WERE AMONG THE FIRST IMMIGRANTS TO FLOW INTO SAN Francisco after word of the gold strike reached their distant shores. Facing immediate prejudice from the people living in the growing city on the bay, they established a district where they could live in familiar surroundings and practice their own customs. In addition, Chinese men headed into the mountains to search for gold, establishing towns like Chinese Camp, in which an estimated five thousand Chinese immigrants lived during the early 1850s.

But life was difficult for these hardworking people. They looked different, ate unusual foods, spoke a strange language, and wore long single braids (queues), all of which created even more suspicion and hatred from the Anglos and other ethnic groups of prospectors.

In 1853, a group of Chinese men, who had been fishermen in their home country, headed south from San Francisco to literally test the waters around Monterey. Besides its beautiful natural bay, Monterey was known for the abundance of fish that swam in its cool waters. These resourceful Chinese planned to set up a commercial fishing enterprise. And the main product for their new business? Squid.

To be clear, squid and octopus aren't fish at all. They're invertebrate cephalopods that provide a popular food source in China, Japan, Italy, and many other countries. Squid were abundant in Monterey Bay. Although no one knew exactly why, these odd creatures had chosen the coast of Central California as their favorite spawning ground. Squid congregate around Monterey between the early spring and summer months, laying their eggs in the shallow waters near the shore. There were millions of them just waiting to be harvested, and up to that point, no one had tapped into the potential squid market.

Setting up a village on Point Cabrillo, the men were soon bringing in enough squid not only to supply the population of San Francisco's China-town but also to export the dried food product to their homeland. Huge Chinese junks (ships) could be seen at anchor in Monterey Bay much of the year. They brought supplies to the Chinese immigrants, items that they couldn't obtain in America. On the return voyages, their cargo holds were filled with dried squid, a product in great demand in China.

The Chinese used an ancient technique for catching squid. Each night, the fishermen rowed their little fleet of sampans into the bay. A basket filled with burning "fat pine" was dangled over the bow of several boats, providing a cumulative glow that was bright enough to attract the squid toward the surface. This method included a sort of squid roundup. While several boats dropped handheld nets, the lighted boats would draw the squid to them, like moths to the flame. The net would be closed in draw-string fashion—until the creatures were trapped.

Of course, this was long before refrigerated transportation, so the squid were salted and dried on wooden pallets. Acres upon acres of dead squid lay baking in the sun all around Monterey—tens of thousands of them in various stages of dehydration. The foul stench was carried by the wind for everyone in Monterey to smell. Understandably, the local residents weren't thrilled about the Chinese squid-fishing business. First, there was the odor. And second, the Chinese hadn't exactly been wel-comed with open arms.

HATRED TURNS TO VIOLENCE

Animosity toward the Chinese had been growing worse through the years. Over time, they were restricted to the type of businesses they could own: generally laundries, certain kinds of shops, and restaurants. Only a few jobs were open to Chinese workers, and they were often too danger-ous for English-speaking men. Thousands of Chinese built the railroads, handled the explosives used in the mines, and blasted tunnels through the mountains.

Although they kept to themselves, lived in their own communities, and worked extremely hard to make ends meet, bigotry boiled over into violence in numerous places in the West. For instance, in 1871, a mob of five hundred white and Hispanic men in Los Angeles killed a total of nineteen Chinese men. Fifteen were hanged, and four others were shot. Some of the men who had participated in the massacre were prosecuted, but their convictions were eventually overturned. They had clearly gotten away with racially motivated murder.

Anti-Chinese sentiment finally culminated in the Chinese Exclusion Act passed in 1882 in an effort to keep these immigrants from continuing to come to the United States. Although the Chinese living in Monterey tried to make peace with the local residents, tensions in the town had been mounting for some time. Seeing how successful the squid fishermen had been, transplanted American fishermen wanted exclusive use of the bay. They encouraged the businessmen who owned the squid-drying fields to terminate the Chinese leases.

In 1906, the final blow occurred when a "mysterious" fire burned Monterey's Chinatown to the ground. Discouraged, most of the Chinese population in Monterey moved to other parts of the state and started over. Those who stayed eventually worked in the Anglo-owned fish factories that would become Cannery Row.

The Exclusion Act was supposed to last for ten years, but it was renewed in 1892 and was made permanent in 1902. The federal law wasn't repealed until 1943.

With the Chinese gone from Monterey Bay, the Americans adopted their technique for squid fishing. Today, fishing boats are equipped with expensive, high-power halogen lights that reach into the depths of the sea. According to the California Department of Fish and Game, Monterey's fishermen bring in an average of 100 tons of squid per night. The area's annual squid catch is 6,500 tons per season (May to November), though in a good year that number can soar to 14,000 tons.

Today, Monterey's squid are frozen and shipped to consumers around the world. As the demand for squid continues to grow, will California's squid eventually be fished out, like so many other types of sea life? Who would have guessed that the alien-looking squid would become one of the California fishing industry's most profitable catches, generating millions of dollars for the state?

If you happen to be in Monterey during squid season, gaze across the bay at night and you'll likely see the eerie green glow of the fishing boats.

Chapter 21

James Lick and the Lick Observatory

BORN IN STUMPSTOWN (LATER RENAMED FREDERICKSBURG), PENNSYL-
vania, in 1796, James Lick lived an amazing life. He had little formal
education and learned to do carpenter's work as an apprentice at a shop
in town. He had fallen in love with a young woman named Barbara Snavely and asked her father for her hand in marriage. Even though she was
expecting Lick's child, her well-off father forbade the marriage because
he didn't think Lick would amount to anything. Brokenhearted, Lick said
good-bye to Barbara and left for Baltimore, Maryland, determined to
find a way to make his fortune and marry the woman he loved.

Portrait of James Lick (ca. 1860).

As a trained carpenter, he took a job making pianos, a lucrative venture at a time when everyone who was anyone owned a piano. The enterprising Lick saw an opportunity to open his own piano store and moved to New York City. Although his business was very profitable, when he received orders from cities in far-off South America, the adventurous American decided to sell his business—lock, stock, and piano—and take a ship to Buenos Aires, Argentina. Although he often said there was too much corruption and crime there, he remained in Argentina for years. By the time he was thirty, he had built a prosperous business that made him a sizable fortune. In fact, he had become so rich that he left his business in the hands of his employees and spent the next year touring Europe.

On his return trip home to Argentina, James Lick's life took a dramatic turn. Sounding like something we'd read in an adventure novel, the ship he traveled on was captured by Portuguese pirates. The crew and passengers were held as prisoners and taken to Montevideo, Uruguay. Whether it was by luck or by wits, Lick managed to escape, walking all the way to Buenos Aires! Perhaps it was because he felt fortunate to be alive that he returned to Stumpstown in 1832, hoping to reunite with Barbara Snavely and their son. After all, he had become a wealthy man. Her father would have to agree to their marriage. But when he arrived, he learned she had married someone else, and his son didn't even know him. In fact, she had married her husband a mere two years after Lick had left for South America. Was this the reason Lick never married?

Returning to Buenos Aires, once again, Lick moved his business—this time, to Lima, Peru. There he met Domingo Ghirardelli, and a friendship developed between them that would change both of their lives.

Although his piano company had provided Lick with a growing fortune, his restless spirit begged for another new adventure. That opportunity presented itself when several of the Mexican craftsmen working at his piano factory quit sometime around 1847 when news that America was about to go to war with Mexico had reached Peru. The American government had decided it was time to claim the southwestern regions of land that had been part of the original Spanish territories.

Lick seems to have had a sixth sense about business opportunities. He was convinced Americans would win the war with Mexico and

President Polk would thereafter take the Mexican territories for the United States. Lick's attention turned to California, a place that had a lot going for it: natural harbors, fertile agricultural valleys, and productive wineries. Port towns had already been established along the coastline. Huge cattle ranches provided meat for the growing populations throughout the region. President Polk would surely make California a state as soon as possible, and James Lick planned to buy as much property there as he could afford.

Selling his piano business in Peru, Lick planned to leave for California. His friend and neighbor, Domingo Ghirardelli, was an excellent chocolate maker. Never missing an opportunity to make money, Lick bought six hundred pounds of Ghirardelli's chocolate bars to sell in San Francisco. In addition, he brought his carpenters' tools and $30,000 in cash and gold (over $1 million today). After selling the chocolate bars in record time, he wrote to Ghirardelli urging him to join him in California. He would be the only chocolatier in the burgeoning city and would be able to make plenty of money if he opened a candy shop there. (For more information, see Ghirardelli's story in chapter 10.)

Lick's lucky streak continued in California, as he arrived shortly before the discovery of gold at Sutter's Mill. His timing was perfect, for that meant he got in on the ground floor of the soon-to-be gold boom. He knew that once the news of California's gold traveled to foreign countries, ships from all over the world would soon arrive in San Francisco. The new arrivals would need places to stay, food to eat, and merchandise to purchase for their trip into the Sierra Nevada Mountains where they were sure they would strike it rich.

Lack of book learning didn't matter when it came to James Lick. He was an intelligent young man with lofty ideas. His predictions about California's future were spot on. The opportunities in the fledgling city exceeded his wildest dreams. And, because of the discovery of gold, it happened amazingly fast. But it wasn't gold that would make his fortune. It was land. After buying real estate in San Francisco, he bought farmland and orchards around the San Jose area, building a large mill to provide flour for the growing population.

His vision didn't stop in Northern California; his holdings extended to Santa Clara Valley, Lake Tahoe, and Nevada. Believing Santa Catalina Island off the coast of Southern California had the potential to become a popular tourist destination, he bought the island in 1864. As his property and real estate holdings grew, so did his vast fortune. While he often stayed at one of his hotels in San Francisco, he built an enormous mansion for himself in Santa Clara. Oddly, he never furnished it but, instead, slept on a door that was laid flat and propped up with wooden supports. Why would he create such a magnificent home and do nothing more to make it a wonderful place to live? Was it because—even with all of his millions—the one thing the land baron didn't have was a family?

He sent for his son, John Woods, whom he had never met. John's mother, Barbara, the woman Lick had never forgotten, had died a few years earlier. The relationship between John Woods and James Lick was strained, though John stayed in California for seven years.

In 1874, the seventy-eight-year-old millionaire suffered a stroke. His mortality had come down on him like a hammer, and he wanted to leave some sort of legacy. How should he spend his fortune? He considered having a huge statue of himself built in San Francisco. Or perhaps a pyramid could be built for him—one that would be taller than the Great Pyramid of Egypt. In the end, he bequeathed a portion of his fortune to Berkeley University to build an observatory named in his honor. Lick donated $700,000 to the university (more than $19 million today) and selected a site on Mount Hamilton east of San Jose for the structure. When it was completed, the observatory would house the biggest telescope west of the Mississippi. It would truly be a marvel, one that made Californians proud. Upon his death, his remains would be buried beneath the structure. And it would, Lick believed, be perfect for his final resting place.

But the observatory hadn't yet been completed when James Lick died at his San Francisco hotel, the Lick House, in 1876. His body was buried at the Masonic Cemetery in San Francisco, where it remained for the next ten years. Lick's remains were moved to the site of the Observatory's Great Refractor telescope, where he was reinterred in its base on January 9, 1887. As he had requested, James Lick lies directly beneath the telescope.

At the time the observatory was constructed, the astronomical observatory "surpassed all others existing in the world." The refracting telescope was the largest that had ever been constructed.

Before signing the final documents for building the observatory, he had made two more stipulations. First, he insisted there had to be a proper road built up the steep mountainside so that the observatory would be accessible to everyone. Second, he asked that fresh flowers be placed at his grave each and every day. For decades, flowers were laid in front of the bronze plaque serving as his headstone. Today, a beautiful artificial floral arrangement decorates the place where Lick lies, although fresh flowers are often left by visitors as a thank you for his generous donation that helped establish the observatory.

Chapter 22

Joaquin Murieta: Man or Myth?

Once upon a time in Old California, the name Joaquin Murieta sent shivers up the residents' spines. According to legend, the Mexican bandit was a cold-blooded killer, a horse thief, and someone you prayed you'd never encounter. But was he real, or was he simply a character in an 1854 novel titled *The Life and Adventures of Joaquin Murieta*, written by San Francisco newspaper reporter John Rollin Ridge, aka Yellow Bird, a Cherokee Indian?

It's possible that Ridge based his main character on the life of a real person who had come to California's Mother Lode country to prospect for gold. There had been stories about a young Mexican miner who had struck it rich, only to have his claim stolen by a group of Anglos who beat and robbed him. Was this the story upon which the author had based his novel, embellishing it to create a more dramatic and romanticized tale of a man's utter revenge upon those who had stolen from him and killed the woman he loved?

In Ridge's story, Joaquin Murieta (spelled with one *r* by the book's author, but often spelled with two) had brought his wife, Rosita, with him from Sonora, Mexico, to California to prospect for gold along the banks of the Stanislaus River. He had filed a legal claim on the land he and Rosita worked, and when they found a gold deposit, word of his strike spread like wildfire. Before long, several drunken American miners attacked Joaquin and Rosita. Joaquin was beaten, and his wife was raped and killed. The men not only stole the gold but also took over Joaquin's

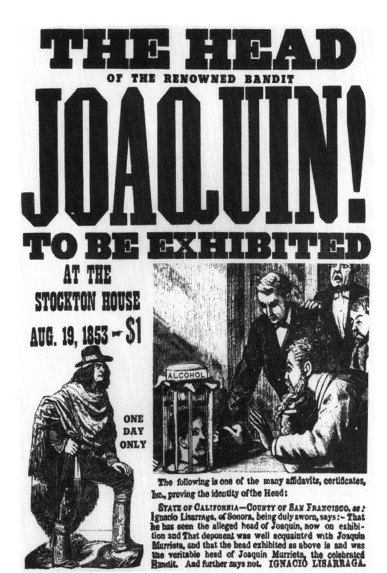

Poster advertising the opportunity to see Murieta's head in a jar (1853).

claim. Despite Murieta's legal ownership of the claim, the court ruled against him, stating that Mexicans who weren't American citizens had no legal right to own property in California.

Penniless, grief stricken, and full of hatred, Joaquin was determined to avenge his wife by killing the men who had murdered her and stolen his gold claim. Not only did he fulfill his promise when he executed the thieves, but he took his vengeance a step further and began stealing from the other miners in the camps. His hatred of the Anglos didn't stop there. Joaquin held up stagecoaches, stole horses, and murdered countless innocent people.

Was it truly Murieta perpetrating all of these crimes, or was it various groups of men looking for ways to become rich off of the miners? If there was a real Joaquin Murieta, was he used as a scapegoat? Ridge's novel was taken as the truth by too many people. But regardless of who was actually committing the robberies, things had become so frightening in Northern and Central California that the governor offered a hefty reward for the capture of Murieta and his gang of Mexican thieves, including Jack Garcia, called Three-Fingered Jack, an infamous criminal who reportedly killed without hesitation.

Captain Harry Love, a former Texas Ranger, and a group of twenty California Rangers were hired to find and kill Murieta and his gang. After chasing them for weeks, the rangers came across a band of Mexican horse rustlers camped on the banks of the Arroyo de Cantua in the San Joaquin Valley. At dawn on July 25, 1853, the posse attacked and killed several of the party, supposedly including Murieta and Three-Fingered Jack.

To make sure they had "proof" of the criminals' deaths, they lopped off the heads of Joaquin and Jack, as well as Jack's three-fingered hand, and took them to the closest town with a saloon. It was a seventy-mile ride in the summer heat, and the heads and the hand had understandably deteriorated. Three-Fingered Jack's head was so badly damaged that they discarded it along the way. When they arrived, Captain Love bought pickle jars large enough for the grizzly trophies and filled them with alcohol as a preservative.

This gruesome display was accepted as irrefutable evidence the notorious Mexican bandits were dead. Captain Love and the rest of the posse received their rewards, and as far as the authorities were concerned, the attacks Murieta perpetrated were over. But what should they do with the head and the hand of the two bandits? The jars containing the macabre remains made the rounds as a curiosity and were displayed in saloons throughout the state. The last time the jars were seen was in San Francisco in 1906, when they were destroyed by the earthquake and ensuing fire that consumed the city.

To this day, the question remains: Did Joaquin Murieta ever exist, or was he a fictional character in John Ridge's novel that was based on a composite of several bandits who lived during the early days of California's history? Since 1853, the year of Murieta's alleged death, rumors and stories about him have flourished. One relates that Murieta took his stolen bounty and returned with it to Mexico, bought a ranch, and lived the rest of his life in relative peace. Another account was provided by a woman who claimed to be Mariana Murieta, the widow of Joaquin Murieta who lived near where the posse killed the bandit. She told everyone she had found his body intact and had buried him under a tree. People who were curious about her tale found the tree with a crudely carved cross on its trunk. Most historians have discounted Mariana's claims, noting that Murieta's wife's name was supposed to have been Rosita. Or is it possible she was his second wife? Yet, there weren't any human remains found in the area around the supposed tree.

While many historians don't believe Joaquin Murieta ever existed, there are credible records of someone called by that name leading his gang into San Luis Obispo to a camp near the mission. The townsfolk were so frightened that they hid in their houses until the "desperados" had left town. Other accounts name him in letters and historic documents, making his existence more likely.

And what about the head staring out from the pickle jar? Newspapers said that while the person who had been decapitated definitely had Mexican features, there was no way to know the true identity of that person. The hand, of course, was easier to identify since it did have Jack's identifying two fingers missing.

As the decades have passed, Murieta's legend has grown. Many Mexican people thought of him as a hero, a sort of Robin Hood robbing rich

Anglo men who had stolen California from Mexico. In fact, some believe Murieta was the basis of the fictional character Zorro. Stories about Joaquin Murieta's life and adventures have not only been dramatized in books, but his character has also been used in plays, television shows, and movies.

There are many reasons why Joaquin Murieta's story is most likely true. First of all, we know the English-speaking men in the goldfields frequently mistreated their Mexican counterparts. Why? Because much of the Mexican population of pre–gold rush California had been first on the scene after Marshall's strike was made public by Samuel Brannan's newspaper. (See Brannan's story, chapter 9.) They already lived in California. Many had been born there. A considerable number had been mining in Southern California, in places like Placerita Canyon where gold had been discovered in 1842, years before John Marshall's discovery on the American River.

Additional Hispanic citizens came to the Sierra Nevada Mountains when word of Marshall's find spread to Mexico and Central and South America. Because their journey to the goldfields was much shorter than the men coming from Europe or from the American South or East Coast by wagon train or by ship, many Mexican citizens had simply arrived sooner to claim more of the areas along the gold-producing riverbeds. Oftentimes, they had brought their wives and children with them, when most of the other foreign miners came alone or with a group of men from their own cultures.

The deluge of mining hopefuls arriving from the American states and various parts of the world changed things for the Mexican miners, many of whom had already panned out substantial quantities of gold from their legally obtained claims. Numerous Americans were outraged the Mexican miners were getting rich. Their resentment became even worse when California became a state in 1850. California, they argued, was now part of the United States, and the gold should belong to its citizens . . . and only its citizens. American gold ore pulled out of American soil was meant by God for the Americans, and that was that.

Their anger led to violence against the foreigners and, in particular, Native Americans and Mexicans. All too often, the Americans forced the

Mexican miners off of their claims, and eyewitness accounts in diaries and journals have documented incidents of lynchings and murders.

Learning about what was happening in the goldfields, California's legislators knew they had to take action. There had to be a way to get rid of the Spanish speakers once and for all. With Americans serving as the new state's legislators, they came up with the perfect way of removing the "unsavory sorts" from the goldfields by passing the Foreign Miners' Tax Act of 1850. The new law would target the foreigners working in the Mother Lode territory by charging them a monthly $20 fee (about $737 today). Of course, the American citizens were exempt. Even though many of the Mexicans who had been the early arrivals had already pulled out enough gold to last them the rest of their lives, those Spanish speakers who arrived months later were allotted much smaller claims. Many of them were eking out barely enough ore to buy food and lodging. The tax legislation had worked. By 1851, hundreds of the Mexican citizens had returned to their home country.

Of course, the other non-English speakers, like the Chinese and French, were also affected by the new law. Hundreds of the French immigrants, ripe from the Revolution of 1848 in France, marched in protest in several towns, including Mokelumne Hill, an event often called "California's French Revolution." They declared their independence and raised the flag of France, refusing to pay the tax collector who had come to town. A posse was sent to Mokelumne Hill to squelch the protest and collect the Frenchmen's tax money. Hearing about the impending violence, the governor quickly stepped in and sent a militia to intercede. Commander William Bradshaw was able to negotiate with the leader of the French brigade, averting a disastrous outcome.

Voices of the French miners were heard by the politicians, and the monthly $20 tax was finally reduced to $3 or $4, depending on which foreigners were paying it. Apparently, the Chinese immigrants, who replaced the Mexicans as the most hated of the foreign population, paid the higher price.

As for the young Mexican men who remained in Northern California, they were angry and filled with hate. They had suffered injustices and cruel treatment by too many of the Americans. They had been abused, harassed, and driven from their legal mining claims. And they had not received any justice from the American law enforcement officers. Seeking revenge, by 1853, many of them had turned to a life of crime. They grouped together in gangs, robbing and killing the whites in the mining camps, as well as attacking towns like San Luis Obispo.

All of this leads one to believe Joaquin Murieta was indeed a real person—a man whose wife had been killed in an attack by American thieves who also stole Murieta's gold and his claim.

Chapter 23
The Strange Case of Emperor Norton

No book filled with stories about Old California's most interesting and unusual people, places, and things would be complete without the story of Joshua Abraham Norton. For those living in the Bay Area, the name is likely familiar. Not only is the legend of Emperor Norton still remembered, but there have been numerous recent attempts to memorialize him by naming the Oakland Bay Bridge for him. Why? While the abundance of admiration for the odd man defies explanation, San Franciscans considered Norton an indescribably colorful character who added charm to their city.

Although the records conflict, it's believed Joshua Norton was born around 1818 in England. His family lived in South Africa for a number of years before Norton moved to San Francisco around 1849. He didn't immigrate penniless, like so many others who packed the developing city. It's believed he arrived with a substantial amount of money to invest in businesses and property.

By 1852, he was already among San Francisco's growing class of wealthy elite. Besides purchasing property, Norton was making a fortune with his investments importing rice. As the years passed, however, foreign traders brought cheaper rice to San Francisco. When the price of rice dropped dramatically, Joshua Norton began to lose his fortune.

The consequences for Norton were terrible, and by 1858 he had lost everything, including his real estate investments. It's believed the shock of his losses caused a mental breakdown. The result was that Norton couldn't accept the reality of being completely destitute. Joshua Norton had been extremely rich, and in his mind, he still was. To say the least, he had serious delusions of grandeur. But things went much further. He created an imaginary world; a world in which he was the ultimate ruler of the entire country.

In 1859, Norton distributed handwritten letters to local newspapers. He roamed the streets and handed his letter of declaration to as many San Franciscans as possible. In his letters, he proclaimed himself "Norton I, Emperor of the United States," adding the title of "Protector of Mexico" shortly thereafter.

At first, everyone believed it was merely a humorous prank by a poor vagrant. As time passed, however, it became apparent that Joshua Norton was serious. Some called him an eccentric, while others regarded him as downright insane, although perfectly harmless. Dressing in a dashing military uniform gifted to him by the officers stationed at the U.S. Army post at San Francisco's Presidio, he patrolled the city's streets, inspecting cable cars, tracks, buildings, roads, and anything he believed was under his supervision. Proud and stiff backed, he expected people to bow to him . . . or at least give him a small dip of the chin and a kind word. His full-dress blue attire included golden epaulets and other regalia, including a long ceremonial saber. And when that uniform became tattered and faded, the city awarded their "emperor" a brand new one.

The amazing thing is that the people of San Francisco didn't seem to mind the odd man or his crazy claims. In fact, he was something of a local celebrity; so much so that local merchants sold souvenirs bearing his name. Even more unbelievable was that "Emperor Norton" issued his own currency, and that it was honored in the many stores and eateries he frequented.

Besides "running San Francisco," Norton considered himself a powerful politician, making announcements and giving decrees that affected the entire country. As the emperor, he believed he had the authority to dissolve the United States Congress, threatening that he would use military force if necessary. He called for abolishing both political parties, citing the reason as the corruption of its members. And when Congress met despite Emperor Norton's demands to the contrary, he summoned the U.S. Army to take action in Washington, DC. Of course, his orders were met with a few chuckles and absolutely no action.

The "Emperor" banned using the word *Frisco*. Anyone he heard using that despicable nickname for his beloved city was issued a warrant requiring them to pay him a $25 fine. Not all his ideas were as crazy. In 1872, he commanded the city's officials to build a bridge across massive San Francisco Bay to Oakland. In yet another proclamation, he wrote instructions advising the U.S. government to form a "League of Nations," an idea that would not be realized until 1920 at the end of World War I.

Emperor Norton dropped dead on January 8, 1880, while out for a stroll along California Street. San Francisco's favorite and strangest resident was buried in the cemetery at Colma. Around ten thousand people lined the city's streets for his funeral procession.

Joshua Norton was never really forgotten. Since his death, this unusual man has shown up as a character in books, and more recently, actors have portrayed him in various television programs. A plaque dedicated to the eccentric emperor was made in 1939 and is now located in the city's Transit Center. After a petition by a group of dedicated Norton fans was circulated calling for the Oakland Bay Bridge to be renamed the "Emperor Norton Bridge," a trust was set up for a future resolution to be passed by local officials. The outcome is still pending.

Chapter 24
Confederate Sympathizers in California

ON APRIL 15, 1865, PRESIDENT ABRAHAM LINCOLN WAS ASSASSINATED by John Wilkes Booth at Ford's Theater in Washington, DC. When the terrible news traveled over the wires to Los Angeles, California, Southerners living in the area celebrated in the streets. During this "demonstration of joy" by the pro-Confederate sympathizers, troops were dispatched to the city from Camp Latham (near today's Culver City) to restore order. Provost marshals were authorized to arrest the demonstrators, who were considered "accessories after the fact" in the assassination plot. The pro-Union *Los Angeles Tri-Weekly* newspaper strongly denounced the action, writing that the cowards who rejoiced in the death of the president deserved to be hanged. Fortunately, the military presence in the city squelched the revelry, and no hangings were reported.

The Drum Barracks in Wilmington (ca. 1863).

Californians who supported the Union mourned with the Northern states, condemning the actions of "those who showed so little humanity that they would celebrate the death of a president." On the day of Lincoln's funeral, schools, banks, government buildings, and most businesses were closed throughout the Southland out of respect for the fallen president.

A procession of Angelenos marched through the streets of downtown to city hall, where a service was held to honor President Lincoln. Participants came from all walks of life and included various religions and ethnicities. The culmination of the march was a nondenominational service held at city hall. Churches and synagogues all over Southern California held special services.

By the early 1860s, more than half of the population of Los Angeles had come from the Confederate states. Most of the pro-slavery residents who moved to Southern California had brought with them their love of the land, agriculture, and, unfortunately, their political and philosophical beliefs regarding slavery.

As early as 1849 when Californians had applied for statehood, a debate raged as to whether slavery should be allowed. Fortunately, the antislavery voices were loud and clear, outnumbering those who advo-

Bella Union Hotel in downtown Los Angeles (1873).

cated this inhumane practice. Slavery simply would not be tolerated in California.

But the pro-slavery factions didn't give up that easily. They formed secret societies, meeting covertly to plan ways to divide California into two sections, so that Southern California could become part of the pro-slavery coalition. Their goal was to eventually include the entire American West among the states allowing the immoral institution of slavery.

In 1859, these powerful men even went so far as to pass legislation by a two-thirds majority vote to create a separate Southern California. As the debate continued, Congress stepped in to prevent this from happening. That occurred around the beginning of the Civil War on April 12, 1861, when rebel forces fired upon the Union garrison at Fort Sumter in North Carolina.

For years tensions had been increasing between the Northern and Southern states, and now the war was officially under way. What would far-away California's role become? Would it side with the Union or with the Confederacy? California entered the Union as a free state, much to the chagrin of its many pro-slavery politicians and citizens. But could it remain loyal to the Northern states when so many of its residents were Confederate sympathizers?

Meanwhile, martial law was declared in Los Angeles. General Albert Johnston, commander of the Military Department of the Pacific, was in charge of bringing troops into Los Angeles to keep things calm. It must have been a difficult duty for Johnston to perform, as he was from the South and believed in the Confederate cause. Being an honorable man, however, the general set aside his personal beliefs and led his troops into the city. The federal government knew the only way to keep the local pro-secessionists under control would be to establish a firm Union presence in the Los Angeles area. A military facility known as the Drum Barracks was built in New San Pedro (later known as Wilmington), where some seven thousand soldiers were trained over the course of the next several years. These Union troops guarded roads, wagon trains, and mail routes not only in California, but throughout the Southwest. Several other military posts were constructed around Los Angeles, including one at the Isthmus on Santa Catalina Island. Though it has been remodeled through the years, the building that once housed Union troops still stands and is currently being used as a yacht club.

Why was a fort built in Wilmington and not in the heart of downtown Los Angeles? Even though the port in nearby New San Pedro (later known as the Port of Los Angeles) was still in its infancy, it had to be safeguarded from saboteurs. Many of the ships carrying food, supplies, trade goods, and military personnel around Cape Horn to the Union army's docks on the East Coast were loaded in San Pedro. The port was important . . . which was another reason the Confederacy desperately needed to bring California into its fold.

The Bella Union Hotel in downtown Los Angeles had long been a favorite meeting place for Southern sympathizers. While the Southern gentlemen played billiards, drank the finest liquor in the city, and smoked the best cigars money could buy, they plotted to find ways to take Los Angeles and the rest of Southern California for the Confederacy. At the beginning of the war, the hotel was closed, as it was known to be "notorious for sedition." It wouldn't be opened again for several years.

This didn't stop the supporters of the Confederacy. They tried to recruit General Albert Johnston to side with the rebel faction and form a guerrilla army to seize federal installations in Southern California. Johnston had resigned his position but refused to betray the trust he had been given as a general. He even continued with his job until a Union replacement arrived. Eventually, he went East and joined Robert E. Lee's forces. He was killed fighting for his beliefs. Without Johnston's leadership, and with the tightened controls in Los Angeles, the Confederacy's hope of seizing the western frontier soon faded.

While the majority of Old California's population consisted of Southern Democrats, including John Downey, who served as the state's governor during the early years of the Civil War, monetary support and troops went to assist the Union army. Many of the state's officials were against slavery, and legal battles had been settled in the enslaved person's favor. (See Biddy Mason's story, chapter 13.)

And yet, for years the Southern sympathizers—both civilians and politicians—continued to help their cause. Confederate forces needed financial support, and California had become rich with gold. What better way to find gold without all the work of digging for it than to rob the stagecoaches carrying sacks of gold to places like Placerville and Sacramento where the boxes holding the bullion could be held in banks or shipped to the new mint in San Francisco.

Stagecoach robberies became commonplace. The thieves were heavily armed, and shootouts between the robbers and guards often resulted in deaths on both sides. In numerous cases, men who supported the Confederacy were responsible for the robberies. It was their way to get money to support the Confederate cause, and it cost many of them their lives.

Meanwhile, the battle for control of the Golden State's future continued. One major event that changed the course of history was the infamous pistol duel between California's U.S. Senator David Broderick, who was an antislavery Republican, and Judge David S. Terry, a pro-slavery Democrat. (See "The Deadly Sharon Scandal," chapter 30.) In the aftermath of Broderick's death at the hand of Terry, numerous Californians changed their political views. Countless voters, sick and tired of the slavery issue and furious over Broderick's death, switched their allegiance to the Republican candidate, Abraham Lincoln, rather than electing the pro-slavery Democratic candidate, General George B. McClellan, as the president.

After the war ended, secessionist supporters in Los Angeles couldn't put the so-called Southern cause behind them. Fights and duels between men who supported the South and those who supported the North still erupted, particularly when liquor was involved. One of those duels occurred at the Bella Union Hotel, opened once again and still a place where pro-slavery supporters often gathered.

Andrew J. King, a Southern Democrat who was an avid, outspoken anti-Unionist, served as the undersheriff of Los Angeles County. He made his anger and disappointment in the outcome of the war public knowledge. When King made bitter comments about how he didn't owe his allegiance to the United States government, he made a lot of enemies. He was taken to the office of Colonel James Henry Carlson, who forced him to pledge his allegiance to the Union. When King finally complied, he was released.

But that wasn't the end of the matter. A feud between King (and his family) and Colonel Carlson would end up in a deadly duel with pistols. King had no intention of kowtowing to the Unionists or James Carlson. The friction carried into a ball held in Los Angeles in July 1865, where Carlson and King had a verbal exchange leading to a fight between them. The story goes that the colonel injured King, who was left with a gash over his heart and an injured hand.

The following day, two of King's brothers followed Colonel Carlson into the saloon at the Bella Union Hotel and began shooting. Carlson shot back. One of King's brothers, Frank, was killed. The colonel was shot by Houston King, the second brother, and died of his wounds. Houston was arrested on the charge of murder but was eventually acquitted.

Even though California had never been at the center of the Civil War, the state played a significant role in the Union's victory. By the end of the war in 1865, California had provided more than fifteen thousand volunteer troops to serve in the Union army and more than $1,200,000 to purchase supplies and weapons. A portion of California's money also supported wounded Union soldiers through the Sanitary Commission, an organization similar to the Red Cross.

As time passed, the Civil War and the animosity between California's Confederate and Union supporters became a distant memory. And today, most people don't realize the important role California played in the war between the states.

Chapter 25

James Reavis: The Prince of Swindlers

JAMES ADDISON REAVIS, THE "PRINCE OF SWINDLERS," PULLED OFF ONE of the greatest land fraud schemes in history. The scam was so impeccably planned and so flawlessly executed that it took more than a decade for U.S. government investigators to uncover it.

Born in 1843, James Reavis grew up on a farm in rural Missouri. When the Civil War broke out in 1861, he was eighteen years old. Like other young men in the South, he was inducted into the Confederate army. In the early months of the war, Reavis seemed to be an enthusiastic soldier. As time passed, however, the horrors of fighting, the reality of the bloody battles, and constant death must have taken a terrible toll on

James Reavis, not looking so princely in his prison stripes (1895).

Reavis, for he began thinking about ways to get out of his conscription. Clearly, serving as a soldier wasn't what he envisioned for himself.

That's when his life of crime began. Successfully forging documents on numerous occasions, he used his newly acquired talent to create his own furlough papers and made his escape. His plan worked, but in a strange twist, he wound up surrendering to the Union forces not far from the Confederate encampment where he had been stationed. Even odder is that he was assigned to an artillery regiment fighting against the Confederate troops. Using his wits to get out of his latest predicament, Reavis came up with the story that he needed a leave of absence to get married.

Of course, there was no bride-to-be, and when he received permission from his commanding officer to take time off to have the nuptials performed, he managed to hightail it to Brazil. If he had stayed in the South, there was a good chance he would either be captured by the Union or the Confederate armies and charged with desertion. Living in Brazil and taking odd jobs was a much safer proposition than staying in America while the Civil War raged on.

Once things had settled down, James Reavis returned to the United States, settling in St. Louis. This time, he tried selling real estate. He had an instinct for wheeling and dealing and must have been a convincing salesman, as he became quite successful. The money he made allowed him to speculate in property investments. As time passed and the money rolled in, Reavis owned chunks of land around St. Louis. Whether or not the transactions were all legitimate is questionable, but in the end, he had become wealthy.

His life took a pivotal turn when he met George M. Willing Jr., a former doctor turned con man, whose racket involved claiming bogus Spanish land grants. He must have seen Reavis's potential as a master thief and forger, as Willing cut him in on a deal that Willing believed would secure the two men a fortune in Arizona land.

With Reavis at the helm, the hoax the pair concocted was nothing less than genius. While doing research to locate old Spanish land grants in Arizona, Willing found a Spanish nobleman, Don Miguel de Peralta, who had been the recipient of the land grant from the king of Spain in 1744. Willing came up with a story claiming Peralta's last descendant had been a friend of Dr. Willing's. Because the last of the Peraltas had died without any progeny, Willing would legally declare the nobleman had left everything to him.

In a twist of fate, Willing died in 1874 while gathering old documents relating to the Peralta Spanish land grant, twelve million acres that included the towns of Phoenix, Mesa, and Tucson, Arizona. The Santa Fe Railroad's tracks ran through the Peralta land. The Silver King mine and numerous rich copper ore deposits were part of the vast property. Whoever could lay legal claim to the Peralta land grant would be rich beyond their wildest dreams.

Meanwhile, James Reavis married a young woman named Ada Pope. A short time later, Reavis left his wife behind in St. Louis and headed west to Downey, California, where he landed a job as the principal of a local school. Did he have the education or experience needed for this position? Could it be that Reavis used forged documents to authenticate his nonexistent references? He was, after all, a man of amazing intelligence who could seemingly convince people of just about anything. And why did he marry Ada Pope and leave her behind in Missouri instead of taking her to California?

As if this story isn't strange enough, Reavis knew Dr. Willing had died in Prescott, Arizona, in 1874. And yet, he made no attempt to locate the treasure trove of Peralta documents Willing had gathered—that is, until 1880 when he located them in Prescott. That's when Reavis went to work on his master scheme to claim the Peralta land grant and make himself the sole beneficiary.

With Willing dead, he came up with a different scheme. First, he became an authority on international law, eighteenth-century Spanish legal terms, and colonial procedures. Finally, when the time was right, Reavis traveled to Mexico City where he diligently studied, then forged documents that had supposedly been signed by the king of Spain in 1742. The name he forged on the historic documents as the new owner of the enormous land grant was James Addison Reavis. To further his claim, he traveled to Madrid, Spain, and continued forgeries on historic records. His forgeries were nothing less than genius. The man who had been born on a farm in Missouri and had no formal schooling had taught himself enough Spanish to master translating the aging documents so that he could re-create them to his advantage.

With that accomplished, Reavis decided to take things a step further. In an effort to unquestionably secure himself as the owner of the vast Arizona land grant, he contrived yet another scheme. Reavis would create a so-called "blood relative" who was a "direct descendant" of Don Miguel de Peralta. This part of the scam was a regular Pygmalion story with a devious twist. Reavis groomed Sophia Treadway to assume the role as Sophia, Baroness of Arizona. Once the young woman had been properly prepared to act out her role, Reavis married her and then took her to the courts of Spain where she could be introduced into high society. Reportedly, he had never legally divorced the first Mrs. Reavis, though she later filed divorce papers when she learned her husband had remarried.

While in Spain, Reavis "assisted" his new wife in collecting the lands and money that were "rightfully hers" by forging even more documents and placing them in the dusty vaults where the old records were stored. He soon presented Spanish authorities with an elaborate, falsified family tree, complete with photographs of Sophia's "royal ancestors." Reavis had acquired the photos at a local street market, carefully concocting an illustrious web of deception that made his wife the sole heir to the Arizona lands.

Fooled by Reavis's skill as a forger, the Spanish government verified the documents as valid. After years of work and careful planning, Mr. and Mrs. Reavis, now titled "the Baron and Baroness of the Colorados and Arizona," returned to the United States from Spain and began living a life of luxury. Not only did they collect rents from the railroad, but Reavis received money from the silver and gold mines located on their property. Arizona ranchers and businesses either paid Reavis or they had to forfeit their property. From about 1882 to 1894, the baron and baroness continued their charade. During this time, Sophia gave birth to twin boys, and the millions of dollars kept them living in luxury.

Their bubble burst, however, when U.S. government agents finally proved Reavis was a fraud. In an interview before his death, Reavis stated that his goal had been to become richer than Vanderbilt. If he hadn't been discovered, he believed he would have been worth more than

$100,000,000. To Reavis, it had all been a game. The government agents were his opponents, while the residents and businesses he had duped were merely suckers.

Instead of achieving greatness, Reavis was found guilty of conspiracy in 1896 and lost everything. His money, his reputation, and his family were gone. In typical James Reavis style, he managed to manipulate the system, spending only two years in prison, a sentence most people felt was far too lenient for the magnitude of his crimes. The penniless second Mrs. Reavis divorced her husband and was officially deposed from her royal position by the courts of Spain. Apparently, Reavis had convinced Sophia that her title and land claims were legitimate, and that she was truly the long-lost Peralta ancestor. Shocked and humiliated by the highly publicized scandal and her husband's lies, she and the Reavis twin boys moved to Denver, Colorado.

After James Reavis was released from jail, he returned to Southern California, where he attempted to get back into the land-selling business with imaginative get-rich-quick schemes. But Reavis was now known as the infamous "prince of hornswogglers." No one was about to be taken advantage of by the con man this time. Failing miserably at everything he tried to do, he was destitute and in failing health. With no one to care for him, seventy-year-old James Reavis entered the Los Angeles County Poor Farm in 1913.

Reavis was dying. He longed to see his ex-wife and sons before his death. He was released from the County Farm and, using public funds, headed for Denver. When he died in 1914, James Addison Reavis, the Prince of Swindlers, the man who was once worth an unimaginable fortune, was buried in a pauper's grave in Denver.

Chapter 26
Lost Treasure of the Hollywood Bowl

BY THE TIME THE HOLLYWOOD BOWL FIRST OPENED IN 1922, THE LEG-end of the gold and jewels buried beneath the acreage of the now-famous landmark had been all but forgotten. The story of the treasure of the Hollywood Bowl dates back to 1866, when Emperor Maximilian ruled Mexico. According to legend, three disgruntled aides to the emperor stole a fortune from the government's treasury in Mexico City. The sto-len loot was hidden in various types of containers and carried north into California on mules. Eventually, they arrived in what is now San Bruno near San Francisco. Weary from the trip and in need of rest before trying to sell any of the valuable items, they buried the plunder to keep it safe. After tethering the pack animals, the men mounted their horses and set off toward the town.

What they didn't realize was that a poor shepherd, a young man from a tiny village in Mexico, was watching from behind a tree. When they were a safe distance away, the lad dug up the cache: two small wooden chests, numerous bulky leather pouches, and porcelain vases filled with coins, ornate gold and silver jewelry, as well as loose diamonds, pearls, rubies, and emeralds.

This was the answer to his prayers. If he could get the stash back to his village in Mexico without being discovered, he and his family would be rich. Not knowing how soon the men would return, the shepherd loaded up the mules and headed south.

Undoubtedly worried that the threesome would soon be in pursuit, he pushed himself and the animals to the limit. Fortunately, the thieves never caught up with him. Did they meet with an untimely demise somewhere? Were they caught by authorities who had been in pursuit of the treasure?

Several weeks later, the young man finally reached the Cahuenga Pass on the outskirts of Los Angeles, still a dusty little pueblo. He was exhausted and didn't feel well, so he decided to do what the thieves had done—bury the treasure. Only, he made sure no one was around to see where he hid it. Leading the animals up a ridge, he stopped at a grove of ash trees, dug six deep holes, and filled them with the gold and jewels. Why six? Apparently, that was easier than digging one huge hole, and given his physical state, it was likely all he could manage. Next, he marked the spot by carving his initials into a large tree, just in case.

Hobbling the animals in the thick grass, he headed to a nearby tavern in search of food and rest. What happened next is where the legend of the treasure's curse begins. What we do know is that the young shepherd died the next morning. The tavern's manager, Jesus Martinez, had taken the ailing youth to his own home to help him. Shortly before the young Mexican died, he told Martinez about the buried treasure. Martinez had given the story little credence, since the young man had been delirious with a fever in his final hours.

And yet, through the years, the story continued to haunt Martinez. Finally, curiosity got the better of him. He told a trusted friend, José Corea, about it, and the two men headed off to investigate. Shortly after they climbed the hill and located the dead shepherd's initials carved in the ash tree, Martinez collapsed and died. Had the treasure claimed another victim? Terrified, Corea fled and didn't speak about the incident for the next fifteen years.

Corea must have been stunned when he heard that a shepherd's dog had dug up one of the treasure-filled leather pouches in 1880. Word of the valuable find had swept through Los Angeles like wildfire. Before that time, he never knew for certain if Martinez's story about the treasure was true. There were supposedly six holes filled with riches. The dog had found only one . . . which left five undiscovered pits. But the entire area around the Cahuenga Pass was now privately owned. If he were caught digging on someone else's property, he would be arrested. And yet, he couldn't get it off his mind.

A couple of months later, Corea sneaked up the hill to see if he could find the treasure. Unfortunately, the landscape looked quite different. The trees had been removed, and the property had been planted with crops. Because he had no idea where to look, Corea gave up.

A few years later, José Corea, who had become a lawman in the growing, rough-and-tumble town of Los Angeles, was killed in the line of duty. Was it a result of the curse of the lost treasure?

Is the treasure still there, or was it scooped up—unnoticed—by earthmoving equipment and mixed into the tons of dirt that were removed when the Hollywood Bowl was constructed? Perhaps the man who owned the land on which the first treasure-laden pouch was found decided to do a bit of digging on his own. If he found the remaining five caches, he certainly kept it quiet . . . which would have been a wise thing to do in that era of lawlessness.

Even more intriguing is the idea that the treasure might still be in the ground somewhere near the Hollywood Bowl patiently waiting to be discovered.

Chapter 27

Mary Ellen Pleasant: Mother of California's Civil Rights

ALMOST A CENTURY BEFORE ROSA PARKS'S BRAVE ACT OF DEFIANCE SET the stage for national integration, Mary Ellen Pleasant filed a landmark lawsuit against a San Francisco streetcar company in 1866 for racial discrimination after one of their drivers refused to pick her up because she was African American. While most of the "coloreds" in the area were too poor to fight these racially motivated, unfair practices, Pleasant had both the financial means and the guts to take the North Beach & Mission Railway to court. She believed that everyone, no matter what their color, had the right to ride instead of walk. The court agreed, awarding her $500

Mary Ellen Pleasant (ca. 1904).

in damages. Two years later, however, the State Supreme Court removed the financial damages, although they upheld their original decision to eliminate this kind of bigotry. Still, the amazing woman with the determination of a lioness forever changed California's racial barriers.

How, then, did Mary Ellen Pleasant become wealthy and independent in a world a mere generation away from legal slavery? She was a woman. She was African American. And she never received a formal education. Yet, for a while, she was one of the richest people in California.

The records of Mary Ellen Pleasant's life, including her autobiography, are filled with contradictions and unanswered questions. One of the things historians agree upon is that she studied under the master of all voodoo queens, Marie Laveau, while living in New Orleans. In fact, local newspapers often referred to her as "the Voodoo Queen of San Francisco." No matter how she felt about the label, she didn't keep her beliefs a secret, as she practiced voodoo throughout her life. That only added to her controversial reputation.

Although some of her biographers believe she was born to slave parents in Georgia in 1814, Mary Ellen said in a deathbed interview that she was born as a free person in Philadelphia. Her father was a Kanaka (Hawaiian), and her mother had been a slave in Louisiana. When Mary Ellen was about the age of ten, her parents sent her to live with a Quaker woman in Massachusetts. Remarkably, she never received a formal education, although she did learn to read and write. It was during this time she became involved in the Underground Railroad, a network of people (both white and African American) who helped enslaved people escape from the South.

Pleasant's first husband, James W. Smith, was an abolitionist, a wealthy biracial man who inherited a Virginia plantation from his white father. When Smith died four years after their marriage, Mary Ellen continued their life's work rescuing slaves. Eventually, she married another abolitionist, John Pleasant, but he, too, died. We know she continued to fight against slavery, and in 1859, she donated a sizable amount of money to John Brown, the abolitionist who led the famous raid on Harpers Ferry, Virginia.

From here, the details get even more hazy. Pleasant was a high-profile guide on the Underground Railroad. When she became a hunted fugitive, she headed west rather than face arrest. Another version of her story relates that, after the discovery of gold in California, she saw an opportunity to parlay her money into a fortune in San Francisco, as the burgeoning city was in the throes of the gold boom.

Arriving in San Francisco by ship sometime between 1852 and 1859, two affluent families hired Pleasant to cook, where she earned a whopping $1,000 a month. It's possible she also spent a great deal of time eavesdropping on conversations between her employers and their successful friends to learn the ins and outs of investing. Before long, she covertly used her earnings to buy real estate and to speculate in gold and silver. By the late 1860s, she was reportedly the richest African American woman in the country. Some have speculated her worth was as much as $30 million. That was a mind-staggering amount in those days—and certainly a princely sum for a woman, any woman, to have acquired by her own cleverness, hard work, and brains.

As the years passed and the city's population soared, Pleasant opened numerous successful restaurants, a chain of laundries, and several lavish boardinghouses. She bought property and several houses for both white and African American friends. Not only did she help former slaves with their finances, but Mary Ellen also hired them as employees in her business establishments.

Attempting to keep a low profile, she wanted people to believe she was merely a maid. Claims that Mary Ellen managed her businesses in the guise of a housekeeper are backed up by the odd story about Pleasant's thirty-room mansion on Octavia Street. Although she had the house built with her own money, she invited her silent partner in several business ventures, Thomas Bell, to live with her. San Francisco's high society wagged their vicious tongues. A white man living with a "colored" woman? Mrs. Pleasant practiced voodoo, they said, and nothing good could come of her or her "evil ways." Rumors swirled that the strange woman bewitched the miner-financier or slipped him one of her potions.

Speculation about the pair's relationship ended years later when Pleasant introduced Bell to her long-time friend, Teresa Clingan. The couple was married, and for some unknown reason, they lived with the so-called Voodoo Queen for another two decades.

The worst scandal of Mary Ellen's unusual life occurred in 1892, when Thomas Bell fell down the stairs inside the mansion and died. For years, hundreds of newspaper articles had been written about Mary Ellen's every move. Now, they ran full-page stories accusing her of being a witch who used magic, charms, and love potions to get whatever she wanted. They alleged she committed murder and that she gave Thomas Bell port wine laced with drugs and pushed him over the railing.

Teresa Bell, the grieving widow, apparently believed Pleasant was responsible for her husband's death, though there was no evidence to support the accusations. Teresa filed a civil lawsuit, claiming property rights to the mansion. It's not surprising that Pleasant, a woman of color who was reviled by many San Franciscans, lost the legal battle. Besides handing the mansion over to Mrs. Bell, it cost Mary Ellen tens of thousands of dollars in attorneys' fees.

Mary Ellen Pleasant's name was also associated with Senator William Sharon's sensational divorce case in 1884, when she testified as a witness for her friend, Sarah Sharon. (See "The Deadly Sharon Scandal," chapter 30.) Because of her skin color, many San Franciscans called her "Mammy" Pleasant, a name she hated. Others continued to refer to her as the Voodoo Queen.

Her story ended sadly. When she died in 1904, Mary Ellen was nearly penniless. Her friend, Sarah Hill Sharon, wound up living in a mental institution. The woman who married her friend, Thomas Bell, now owned the mansion she had built. Mary Ellen Pleasant's dying request was that the words "She was a friend of John Brown's" be inscribed on her headstone. She died at the age of ninety and was buried at Tulocay Cemetery in Napa, California. Her gravesite has been designated as a "Network to Freedom" by the National Park Service.

In the 1970s, Mary Ellen Pleasant's extraordinary story was rediscovered. She is now called "the Mother of Civil Rights in California," and several versions of her life have been told in documentary films, books, and even in stage productions. The San Francisco main library has had exhibits and artifacts about her, and a plaque dedicated to her memory was placed in a small park near where her mansion once stood at the southwest corner of Octavia and Bush Streets in San Francisco.

Chapter 28

"If You Will, You Can": The Story of Ng Poon Chew

THROUGHOUT HISTORY, THERE HAVE BEEN BRAVE INDIVIDUALS WHO HAVE defied traditional roles, challenged laws, and risked harassment, imprisonment, and even death to make changes for the better. One such man was named Ng Poon Chew, who was born in China on March 14, 1866.

Ng Poon Chew's grandmother had hoped he would enter the Buddhist priesthood. But the precocious boy had his own ideas, believing his destiny lay outside of China. At the young age of seven, he begged his

Ng Poon Chew (1920).

family to let him accompany his eldest cousin to California. Ng's grandmother said, "If you will, you can," a phrase that became Ng's lifelong motto.

The two Chinese youths arrived in San Francisco in 1873 and made their way to San Jose where there were jobs for Chinese workers. Ng was a bright child and found work as a houseboy, while his cousin obtained a job tending fruit orchards. Eventually, Ng was taken in by a kind white woman who directed the Chinese Presbyterian Mission. It was here he received an education, became fluent in English, and studied the Bible. After converting to Christianity, the young man decided he wanted to become a minister. As the years passed, Ng became a charismatic leader in San Francisco's Chinatown.

Despite the continued harassment of the Chinese, Ng Poon Chew believed it would one day be possible for his people to achieve equality in America, a land filled with immigrants. Ng was a voracious reader, studying both Chinese and American history and politics. Emulating his hero, Theodore Roosevelt, he dressed in Western clothing, cut off his queue (a long braid, dubbed a "pigtail" by whites), and grew a thick walrus mustache. He encouraged other Chinese planning to stay in America to adopt the ways of the Western world, while continuing to embrace their own culture. China was their homeland, their bloodline. But if they were ever to achieve success in this vast melting pot, they would need to adapt.

The progressive Ng lectured to his people whenever possible, discussing not only the Bible but also political and social topics that affected the Chinese population both here and abroad. The biggest issue of that time period was the Chinese Exclusion Act, passed in 1882, which prohibited more Chinese immigrants from coming to the United States. (See "Chinese Squid Fishermen and the Exclusion Act," chapter 20.) Ng worked tirelessly to have this new law abolished.

Around 1890, Ng Poon Chew moved to Los Angeles, serving the local Chinese community as a Presbyterian minister. Angered by the unfairness of singling out the Chinese while other nationalities continued to flood into the country, Ng decided his dialogues would reach a larger audience through the written word. In 1899, he founded *Hua Mei Sun Po*, the first daily Chinese newspaper in the country.

Ng relocated to San Francisco a year later, where he had more contacts within the Chinese and American communities. Renaming his newspaper *Chung Sai Yat Po* (the Chinese American Daily News), he never missed an issue until April 18, 1906, when the infamous earthquake and fire destroyed much of San Francisco.

Not only did he lose all of his equipment and records, but the book manuscript he had just completed about Chinese-American relations was burned. Showing his usual courage, Ng sent to Japan for new machinery—Chinese characters couldn't be reproduced with American printing presses. Meanwhile, he hand-wrote the ensuing issues until the printing presses arrived weeks later.

Although Ng Poon Chew helped rebuild San Francisco's Chinatown, he permanently relocated his newspaper offices, along with his wife and five children, to Oakland. Using *Chung Sai Yat Po* as his mouthpiece, Ng's political editorials continued to inform and influence the Chinese American community for fifty years.

"The newspaper is the people's tongue," he often said. But "the people's tongue" was in Chinese. Ng needed to address the issues of Chinese immigration to the American people. His background as a minister had given him the confidence to lecture before large audiences. His quick mind, mastery of the English language, and a good sense of humor made him a sought-after speaker. Often called the "Chinese Mark Twain," Ng crisscrossed the country on his lecture series. He reached the pinnacle of his success when he addressed the House of Representatives and was invited to the White House to interview Theodore Roosevelt. Deeply moved by Ng's words, the president issued an executive order to the Immigration Service, demanding that it discontinue its abusive treatment of the Chinese. Nothing ever came of Roosevelt's orders, and the situation remained the same.

Although Ng's hopes were continually dashed, he slowly chipped away at American prejudices against his people. His own children attended the university in Berkeley. Each achieved success and broke down barriers, emulating their father's beliefs that all men (and women) were created equal. His eldest daughter was the first Chinese American admitted to public school, and his son, Edward, was the first Chinese American to receive a commission in the U.S. Army during World War I.

By the time of his death in 1931 at the age of sixty-five, Ng Poon Chew had accumulated a great deal of wealth. More important, he had effected countless positive changes for his people, though it would be more than another decade before the Chinese Exclusion Act was repealed.

Breaking down more racial barriers, he had been accepted into the prestigious organization of the Masons and had reached their highest rank. In 1912, Ng was asked to represent China as vice counsel in San Francisco. He was one of the most well-known Chinese people in the United States; he met not only with several American presidents but also with famous Chinese leaders, like Sun Yat-sen, who led a revolution to rid China of its old feudal system.

Chinese Americans credited Ng with the country's growing respect for the Chinese, as well as America's awareness of their struggle against violent prejudices and disregard of their rights as human beings. It had been his life's work, his dream. In 1943, twelve years after Ng's death, the "Great Wall" that divided China and the United States came crashing down with the repeal of the Chinese Exclusion Act.

Chapter 29

The Hat Ranch

PASSENGERS BOARDING ONE OF THE CRUDELY BUILT "MUD WAGONS" IN the town of Mojave were in for a bumpy ride. The lightweight stagecoaches offered none of the usual comforts found on the big Concord stagecoaches, like padded seats and leaf-springs, to help with the bouncy ride. The road leading north from Mojave to the desert towns and mining camps along the southern shoulder of the Sierra Nevada were scarred with ruts and potholes. Because of the oppressive heat, the leather curtains were rolled up and tied, so there was nothing to protect the riders from the incessant winds and blowing grit.

As the driver climbed to his seat and snapped the reins, the wooden coach lurched forward. "Ladies and gents, hang on to your hats," he called down to the passengers. And he wasn't kidding. The "Mojave Zephyrs" were known to blow so hard they could reach gale force. Even on a good day, the wind swept down from the Tehachapi Pass, blowing dust and debris across the desert floor straight into the path of the Mojave stage. More often than not, the zephyrs laid claim to the riders' Stetsons, bonnets, sombreros, fancy ladies' hats with netting and feathers, fedoras, derbies, or any other headgear the wearer might have donned that day. Wigs and toupees were no exception!

When the hats blew out the window, the driver refused to stop the coach. Nothing slowed him down. His schedule was tight, and losing hats was far less important than getting the horses and mail to the next destination. Besides, once the notorious zephyrs got hold of a hat, no one could run fast enough to catch up with it. The hats bounced along like tumbleweeds until they were blown into an area located in a depression near what is today the Mojave Airport. That's the direction the wind always blew. And that's where countless hats of all shapes, sizes, and colors wound up.

Legend has it that whenever the local residents needed new headgear, they would make a trip to the "Hat Farm" to find a style and fit that suited them. Tangled among the sage was a full array of hats from which to choose. The owner of Mojave's haberdashery took advantage of the "windfall" by giving children a few pennies to gather the best of the crop of hats to sell at his store. Passengers losing their hats when leaving Mojave often complained that they had to buy it back from the sly merchant upon their return to town.

Long gone are the days of the uncomfortable mud wagons and the pitiable passengers who had to ride in them. Today, people exploring the area claim they occasionally find tiny scraps of the Hat Ranch's former harvest.

Chapter 30

The Deadly Sharon Scandal

THE "KING OF THE COMSTOCK," WILLIAM SHARON, MADE A FORTUNE in the silver mines of Virginia City, Nevada, in the 1860s. His investments in railroads and California real estate continued to increase his wealth to a staggering amount estimated to be in the multimillions. He accomplished his next goal in 1875 when he was elected as a United States senator.

That same year, Senator Sharon's business partner, real estate mogul William C. Ralston, died of what was presumably suicide when his body was found near North Beach floating in the bay after suffering devastating financial losses. Though he continued serving as senator, Sharon

Photo of U.S. senator David Broderick (1859).

left for California, moving into a huge suite at the magnificent Palace Hotel in San Francisco that he had co-owned with Ralston. It was the beginning of a new, quite scandalous life for William Sharon. A widower, he became notorious for womanizing and kept an ample supply of mistresses on the side.

That's when Sarah Althea Hill entered the millionaire's life. She was a beautiful "Southern belle" who had come to San Francisco in the 1870s. Part of the elite social scene, Sarah had inherited a considerable sum of money from her father. According to the local newspapers' gossip columns, Sarah's appetite for the finer things had quickly depleted her nest egg. More likely, it was the outrageously inflated cost of living in San Francisco that gobbled up her money.

The town's social snobs spread the word that Sarah deliberately set her sights on William Sharon because of his massive fortune. Sarah, thirty years younger than Sharon, countered that she had sought him out to ask for his advice regarding her stock investments. While we'll never know the truth, we do know the former senator was smitten by the pretty blonde. He took her under his wide-spread wings, clothing her in the

Photo of David Terry (ca. 1870).

finest gowns, buying her expensive jewelry, taking her to the city's best restaurants, and introducing her as his "little wife" at numerous social events. Sarah was even on his arm at his daughter's wedding.

Sarah was his constant companion for more than three years. But when she caught him having an "adulterous affair," she filed for divorce. The only problem was that the pair was never legally married. Sarah produced a handwritten note she claimed William had dictated to her as a legally binding marriage contract. The note was signed by the senator and dated "25 Aug 1880." There were also handwritten love letters addressed by William Sharon to "My Dear Wife." He countered, swearing they were never married and that the love letters and signature on the marriage note had been forged by Sarah.

The sensational *Sharon v. Sharon* trial (later changed to *Sharon v. Hill*) began in 1884. Newspapers happily reported the sordid details, exaggerating particulars to sell more papers and stimulate additional public interest. The proceedings went on for years, bouncing from court to court in Northern California. Not only was Sarah accused of forging the signature on the marriage note, but Sharon's lawyers also said she had concocted the entire account of their supposed marriage. Yet, there were plenty of witnesses willing to back up Sarah's claims; people to whom the senator had introduced her to as his wife or Mrs. Sharon.

Still, none of San Francisco's high-powered attorneys was willing to represent Sarah in the lawsuit, as it would have meant going up against one of the richest, most powerful men in California.

That's when an attorney named David S. Terry, former justice of the California Supreme Court, took the case. Tired of San Francisco's political and legal corruption, he vowed to fight for Sarah's "honor." The problem was David Terry had a dubious reputation. Although he never served jail time, he had stabbed a notorious member of a vigilante group in 1856. And in an infamous event that likely changed the political history of California, he killed United States senator David Broderick in a duel with pistols. Broderick, who wanted California to remain an antislavery state, had wielded great political influence in California. Terry, on the other hand, was a supporter of the state's Southern Democratic population and believed California—as well as the rest of the West—should allow its residents to own slaves. The situation had become so hostile between Broderick and Terry that they decided to hold a duel. Broderick was shot in the lung, dying a few days later. Many people believed Broderick's pistol had been tampered with, and that the duel had been rigged so that Terry would win. The outcome of the duel had far-reaching results, for in the long run, Broderick's death shifted the bulk of the population's views toward keeping California as a free state.

Besides being hated for killing Senator Broderick, Terry had made enemies throughout his career. And now he was about to become the lead player in one of the state's most famous legal cases.

Sarah Althea Hill/Sharon and David Terry maintained a professional relationship in the early months of the trial. When Terry's wife died of a long-term illness a short time later, his affections turned to his famous client. He won the first trial for Sarah, marrying her a short time later. Meanwhile, an angry Senator Sharon declared he would rather throw all his money in San Francisco Bay than let Sarah have another penny. Determined to have Sarah's win overturned, William Sharon hired another batch of expensive lawyers to contest the court's decision.

Making matters worse for Sarah was her friendship with Mary Ellen Pleasant, sometimes called the "Voodoo Queen of San Francisco." For years, there had been whispers of hexes and love potions provided by "Mammy" Pleasant for Sarah to use to win the court case. The rumor mill went wild with speculations. People said Sarah killed a pigeon, poked it with pins, put it in a satin purse, and wore it as a talisman around her neck to facilitate the magic charm. Sarah's critics also claimed that when Sarah was trying to win Sharon's affections years earlier, Mammy Pleasant suggested a spell for her. They said that Sarah paid a gravedigger to bury a pair of Sharon's socks in a grave where a body was to soon be interred. When a cemetery watchman came forward to testify as an eyewitness to this strange event, Sarah finally admitted it was true. She explained she believed that if the senator didn't love her by the time the socks rotted, he would die. Needless to say, her reputation was severely damaged by her beliefs in voodoo spells.

Accusations and falsehoods continued to fill the gossip columns. Adding fuel to the fire, the infamous Mary Ellen Pleasant accompanied

Sarah to court each day. When William Sharon suddenly died less than a year later, the newspapers and the public touted the possibility that Sarah's voodoo had something to do with it. Was it stress or black magic that caused his death?

In the end, Justice Fields of the U.S. Circuit Court in San Francisco, a former friend of David Terry's, overturned the lower courts' decision decreeing that William Sharon's signature on the marriage note was indeed forged. Never mind that, in the earlier trial, several neutral handwriting experts had verified it was unquestionably written in Senator Sharon's own hand. But Fields's decision was final, and that was that.

When Sarah shouted that Justice Fields had been bribed by her late husband's representatives, the guards dragged her from the room. Outraged, David Terry pulled a knife, demanding that his wife be released. The guards drew their guns, ready to shoot the lawyer. He dropped his knife and was promptly arrested. He was jailed for six months, while Sarah received thirty days for contempt of court.

Months later, David and Sarah, who had moved to Terry's ranch in Fresno, boarded a train bound for San Francisco. In an unfortunate twist of fate, Justice Fields was also traveling back to San Francisco on the same train. Justice Fields, accompanied by his personal bodyguard, left the train to eat in the restaurant on a layover at the railroad station. David Terry had also headed for the restaurant. Sarah wasn't finished dressing and was a few minutes behind her husband. Entering the eatery, Terry spotted the justice sitting a few tables away. Still angry about the way Justice Fields had treated Sarah in court, Terry approached Fields, yelling at him. When he slapped Fields on the cheek, the justice's bodyguard shot the unarmed Terry twice, mortally wounding him. Moments later, Sarah entered the restaurant and saw her husband bleeding to death on the floor. He died in Sarah's arms.

People who knew Terry said that when he slapped Justice Fields, it would have been nothing more than a challenge to have a duel. Needless to say, Sarah was devastated, and once again, she was alone.

Another huge trial took place later in which the bodyguard was accused of murder. He was eventually acquitted.

Sarah never recovered from David Terry's death. And she never saw any of Senator Sharon's millions. Wandering the streets of San Francisco, she frequently visited the parlors of clairvoyants in an attempt to contact her dead husband. Throughout the rest of her life, she protested that she was legally entitled to a portion of Sharon's estate. The media proclaimed Sarah was crazy, and she was eventually taken to the insane asylum in Stockton, where she remained until her death in 1937.

Chapter 31

City of the Dead: Colma, California

AFTER THE DISCOVERY OF GOLD IN CALIFORNIA IN 1848, SAN FRANCIS-co's population grew at an amazing rate. Many of those arriving by ship had become sick during the long, difficult voyages from their home countries. The voyages took months, and many ships were lost at sea, particularly those sailing around Cape Horn.

Rather than risking a sea voyage, travelers who could afford it often chose taking the faster route, which involved crossing through the jungles of Panama between the Atlantic and Pacific Oceans. These travelers frequently caught malaria, yellow fever, cholera, or a host of other diseases. Poisonous snakes and crocodiles were a constant threat. Those who survived the journey sometimes arrived in San Francisco just in time to die there.

Upon arriving in San Francisco in 1849 or 1850, even those who were in relatively good condition were still at risk for having health problems. The weather was damp, and decent accommodations were few and far between for those who didn't come with a bundle of money. Diseases like pneumonia, cholera, tuberculosis, and influenza claimed countless lives. In addition, robberies, assaults, and murders were an all-too-frequent occurrence in the burgeoning city. The result? Within a few decades, San Francisco's cemeteries were already filled to capacity.

As the area's population continued to swell and property values soared, cemetery business owners sought out nearby areas with cheaper burial grounds. By 1900, with the growing need to use every inch of hilly land for residential and business development, local lawmakers passed a bill prohibiting burials inside city or county lines. Twelve years later, ordinances were also approved stating that the bodies buried in the existing cemeteries would have to be dug up and moved elsewhere. When San Francisco's leaders announced that there would be no more burials in their city or county, it was especially good news for the cemetery businesses in Colma.

Colma (once known as Lawndale) is located nine miles south of San Francisco. The area had been used for agriculture, and land was still plentiful. It could be reached by a main road running clear to San Francisco and was close enough to the Bay Area for funeral parties to comfortably travel between San Francisco and Colma in a single day.

The first graveyard in Colma, Holy Cross Catholic Cemetery, opened in 1887, making it one of the state's oldest memorial parks. Others soon followed, and by the turn of the century, Colma had seven cemeteries catering to various ethnic and religious groups, including the bodies relocated from San Francisco's cemeteries. Another ten cemeteries were eventually opened to accommodate the internment needs of the ever-growing Bay Area population. More than 150,000 bodies were relocated from San Francisco between 1920 and 1941.

Worried that San Francisco would eventually bleed from its boundaries and take over the Colma area, cemetery owners banded together. In 1924, they created the incorporated city of Colma, complete with a mayor and city council. That way, if the big, powerful San Francisco business interests attempted to buy Colma, close the cemeteries, move the bodies again, and use the acreage for housing and businesses, then they would have to go through the city's leaders. Since then, the deceased have rested in peace in tranquil little Colma.

Colma's most unusual—and most visited—cemetery is Pet's Rest. Since it opened in 1947, more than twenty-five thousand beloved animals have been laid to rest in this five-acre parklike setting. Tina Turner's dog is buried there, reportedly laid to rest wrapped in the star's fur coat.

Most old graveyards contain an area known as "Potter's" or "Pauper's Field," a term for the area where the poor or unidentified were buried. You won't find a Potter's Field in Colma, however. It's believed that the area that once served as Potter's Field was incorporated into the seventeen-acre Cypress Golf Course. Reportedly, there are hundreds of people buried beneath the emerald spread of St. Augustine sod, six feet under a beautiful fairway fringed by pine trees and shrubs. Without headstones to mark the graves, or a map marking official boundaries, no one knows exactly where these poor folks lie.

The aboveground residents take a positive approach to their community's rather unusual history. Cars display bumper stickers reading "It's great to be alive in Colma." Rather than referring to their town as the City of the Dead, Colmanians call it the "City of Souls."

The Community and Cultural Center in town includes a local history museum situated in a historic Spanish building, an old railroad depot with displays telling the story of the area's transportation history, a blacksmith shop, and a freight building depicting Colma's agricultural beginnings.

Colma is the only city where the dead outnumber the living by about 1,000 to 1. While there are roughly 1,500 breathing, aboveground residents, more than 1.5 million people can be found underground, interred in one of the city's seventeen cemeteries.

COLMA'S MOST FAMOUS UNDERGROUND RESIDENTS

Many of California's first tycoons and financiers are interred in this historic Necropolis. Levi Strauss, creator of the jeans that bear his name, is buried in Home of Peace Cemetery (est. 1889), one of California's most renowned Jewish cemeteries.

Cypress Lawn Memorial Park (est. 1892) is the city's largest nonsectarian cemetery. Notables buried there include members of the famous Hearst family: Senator George Hearst, his wife Phoebe; and William Randolph Hearst. Claus Spreckels, the sugar baron, lies nearby, as does baseball great "Lefty" O'Doul. William Henry Crocker, one of San Francisco's early movers and shakers, and Charles De Young, founder of the *San Francisco Chronicle* newspaper, are also buried there.

Olivet Memorial Park (est. 1896) contains the remains of Ishi, the last surviving member of California's Yahi Indian tribe. Several members of the infamous Barker gang of crooks are buried there.

Wyatt Earp, famous lawman of the Old West, rests beside his wife in the Hills of Eternity Cemetery. One of Colma's first mayors, Charles Gerrans, is buried there.

Joe DiMaggio is buried at Holy Cross Catholic Cemetery, as is San Francisco mayor George Moscone, who was shot to death by Supervisor Dan White. California's thirty-second governor, Senator James D. Phelan, and A. P. Gianni, founder of the Bank of America, are here, as is Abigail Folger, heiress to the Folger Coffee estate and a lesser-known Manson family murder victim.

One of Woodlawn Cemetery's best-known "residents" is Joshua Abraham Norton, who called himself the "Emperor of These United States and Protector of Mexico." (See Norton's story, chapter 23.)

Chapter 32

A Ghost, a Curse, and Attempted Murder: Mr. Griffith's Park

GRIFFITH PARK'S HISTORY IS SOMETHING STRAIGHT OUT OF A HOLLY-wood movie, complete with a ghost and a curse. The story begins in 1796, when the land that would later include Griffith Park was granted to Jose Vicente Feliz, one of the Spanish soldiers who escorted the forty-four original settlers from Mexico to establish the pueblo of Los Angeles in 1781.

Griffith J. Griffith (1900).

Years later, Jose Vicente Feliz's descendant, Antonio, lived in the rancho's hacienda with his sister, housekeeper, and niece, Petranilla. Life was good for the Feliz family. The cattle had grown fat on the wild grasses that grew in the pastures, and the fertile land had produced abundant crops. Everything changed in 1863. A smallpox epidemic swept through Los Angeles, and Antonio Feliz contracted the disease. He was near death when his lawyer and a friend came to see him at the rancho.

The heirs to Rancho de los Feliz later claimed the pair tied a stick on the back of Antonio's neck, using it to make the barely conscious man nod his agreement to the terms of a new will. It was believed the two beneficiaries named in the revised will were the lawyer and the friend, and that the Feliz family was excluded. Because of this injustice, Petranilla, Antonio Feliz's beloved nineteen-year-old niece, placed a curse on the two men, their descendants, and the land.

These accusations were later refuted when one of the men, the former mayor of Los Angeles, produced a document proving that he purchased the land, though he only paid a mere $1 per acre. Still, the legend of the curse and the ghost of Feliz continued.

Curse or coincidence, from that point on bad luck followed everyone who owned Rancho de los Feliz. There were deaths, murders, fires,

The original Feliz adobe still stands in Griffith Park (2021).
PHOTO BY RICK FLIEDNER.

droughts, floods, and crop failures. One of the later owners, Leon Baldwin, lost his fortune after floods devastated the rancho property, killing the livestock, trees, and crops. Residents of Los Angeles suspected it was because of the curse. And when Baldwin was murdered, no one doubted that it was truly a result of Petranilla's vengeance.

Finally, in 1882 a newcomer named Griffith J. Griffith arrived on the scene and purchased the rancho. At first glance, Griffith seemed to have escaped Petranilla's curse. He made a fortune selling off pieces of the land for development, especially during 1886 and 1887, when Southern California's real estate boomed.

It was around this time that Griffith set his sights on Christina Mesmer, daughter of a rich and socially prominent local family. According to his contemporaries, Griffith was a pompous man, who carried a gold-topped cane and had an annoying, patronizing snicker. On the other hand, he was handsome, wealthy, and charismatic. Christina agreed to marry Griffith and moved to the rancho.

Although the marriage lasted sixteen years, it was an unhappy union. There were numerous failed business ventures, and Griffith soon became as notorious for his alcoholism as he was for his arrogance. By then, he wanted to sell the rancho. But there were no takers.

Instead of selling off more of the property, in 1896 Griffith gifted 3,015 acres to the city for use as a park. People speculated why the "fat little millionaire" would make such a generous donation. Some said it was to get out of paying taxes, while others believed it was because Griffith had been a victim of Petranilla's curse and hoped to placate the angry Feliz spirits.

According to Horace Bell, a famous newspaper reporter who covered the story, the ghost made frequent appearances at the old rancho, including the night when city officials came to the rancho to celebrate Griffith's generous gift to the people of Los Angeles. Bell wrote that the ghost of Antonio Feliz materialized at the head of the banquet table and invited the men to dine with him "in Hell." (Of course, Bell was noted for sensationalizing his articles to sell newspapers.)

If Griffith had made this generous bequest to the people of Los Angeles to appease the old Spanish don and end the famous curse, his efforts failed. Not only did his drinking problem worsen, Griffith became delusional, ranting that his wife was in collusion with the pope to kill him for his money. Suspicious that she had poisoned his food, he switched their plates and glasses when she turned her back. Pacing nervously, biting his fingernails to their quicks, Griffith's hallucinations had become frightening.

In 1903, the situation went from bad to disastrous. Desperate to help her husband, Christina rented the Presidential Suite at a fancy hotel in Santa Monica. Perhaps the cool ocean breezes and soothing sound of the waves would help his deteriorating mental state. It didn't work. Entering the room one day, he carried two items: a revolver and a prayer book. Handing his wife the prayer book, he ordered her to her knees and told her to prepare to meet her maker. She begged for her life, but he had no pity. As he took aim between her eyes, she jerked to one side. The bullet missed its mark, going through her eye. Griffith was about to take another shot when Christina managed to scramble to her feet and jump out the open window. Luckily, she landed in an awning. Though she was severely injured, Christina survived.

The resulting trial was beyond sensational. Despite Griffith's guilt, he only received a two-year sentence in San Quentin, because his attorney came up with a new defense, which he called "alcoholic insanity."

When he left prison, Griffith moved back to Rancho de los Feliz. If the odd man was disliked before he shot his wife, he was now hated by most local residents. Alone and penitent, Griffith decided to give the city fathers $100,000 to build an observatory atop Mt. Hollywood (the name was changed from Mt. Griffith when he was imprisoned). Some sources say they turned down the offer. In 1913, Griffith offered $50,000 to build a Greek-themed theater. And, again, his money was refused. No one wanted to have anything to do with Griffith J. Griffith. Still, he was determined to find a way to bequeath a portion of his fortune to Los Angeles so that the observatory and Greek theater could be built. Upon his death in 1919, Griffith's wish came true. The property and the money needed to build both beautiful structures were the result of this odd man's fortune.

Thanks to Griffith, we now have beautiful Griffith Park, which includes the Los Angeles Zoo, Greek Theater, and the fabulous observatory overlooking the sprawling city. Griffith certainly succeeded in clearing his name with future generations of Angelenos. Few people know the park's curious past or the strange story of the man who made it possible. The ghost of Antonio Feliz seems to have found peace, and Petranilla's wrath has apparently been appeased.

Chapter 33

Tragedy in Tehachapi: The Story of John and Maria Downey

DURING THE LATTER HALF OF THE NINETEENTH CENTURY, JOHN G. Downey was a household name throughout California. His entrepreneurial powers reached far and wide, particularly in the southern portion of the state. He owned businesses and property from downtown Los Angeles to Catalina Island, to San Diego and countless points in between.

John G. Downey, former governor of California (ca. 1870).

Everything he touched turned to gold, bringing him immense fame and fortune. The self-made millionaire had it all—that is, until a blustery night in January 1883, when a terrible accident would forever change Downey's life.

EARLY LIFE

There are several accounts of John Downey's early years. We do know that he was born in Ireland in 1827, and his father died when John was ten. At the young age of fourteen or fifteen, he immigrated to the United States. One version of his life story related that the Irish teenager was a stowaway on a cattle ship. More likely, however, was that he simply paid for his passage by working on a ship heading to America. His eldest brother was seventeen and stayed in Ireland to help their mother.

Arriving in Baltimore, Maryland, where he lived with his uncle and two stepsisters, John attended Latin school, a decision that would later allow him to realize his ambitions by earning a steady, lucrative income as a pharmacist.

At the age of sixteen, he began an apprenticeship as a druggist at an apothecary in Washington, DC. Ironically, at one point in time, he

Maria Bandini Downey, who died in the accident (ca. 1870).

worked with Dr. Samuel A. Mudd, the infamous doctor who rendered medical aid to President Lincoln's assassin, John Wilkes Booth.

The rest of Downey's immediate family finally immigrated to America on the cusp of the Great Potato Famine of 1845. Many of the Downeys' friends, and even a few family members who stayed behind, died of starvation and other related diseases.

LATER YEARS

Downey had a keen mind, worked hard, and did very well at his profession as a druggist. But he wasn't contented and longed to broaden his horizons. He had grand dreams of growing rich in America, the land of opportunity for even the looked-down-upon Irish population.

Leaving Washington, DC, to take a better-paying position at a pharmacy in Ohio, Downey eventually earned enough money to head to California in 1849 to search for gold. But the cost of making the lengthy journey literally ate up most of his savings. When he arrived in San Francisco, he had $10 and a gold pocket watch, which he immediately pawned for $60. That was just enough money to buy his equipment and make the trip to Grass Valley to join the mayhem in the goldfields.

Panning for gold was exhausting—and dangerous. It wasn't long before Downey realized there were far better ways to make a fortune than spending his days panning for nuggets in the freezing river. He packed his belongings and headed back to San Francisco. Always looking for the next opportunity, he worked at odd jobs, saved his money, and headed south to the fledgling pueblo of Los Angeles in 1850. Downey believed the day would come when Southern California would experience the same economic explosion that was happening in San Francisco, and he intended to take advantage of every possible break that he could.

Seeing the need for a pharmacy in the dusty little pueblo town, he teamed up with Dr. James P. McFarland, opening the town's first drug store on Los Angeles Street near the Plaza . . . the only pharmacy between San Francisco and San Diego. Within three years, it had made both men rich.

That was just the beginning for the ambitious Irishman. Downey purchased land . . . and lots of it. He financed private loans at high interest rates, foreclosing on the property owners who couldn't make their payments. In 1859, he and his partner, Dr. James P. McFarland, foreclosed on the former Rancho Santa Gertrudes, a substantial chunk of acreage that had once been part of the enormous Nieto land grant.

After buying out McFarland, who had decided to return to the East Coast, Downey sold much of the property in smaller plots to farmers, thus creating the City of Downey. Another one of Downey's new developments was Los Angeles' first suburb, Lincoln Heights.

Downey was responsible for many other Southern California "firsts." For example, he built the first two-story house in town, a mansion located on Main Street between 3rd and 4th Streets. Although Los Angeles was in the throes of expansion during the 1870s, the town didn't have a formal bank. Downey knew that the old barter system still used at that time simply had to go. After he found financial backing, he and another partner opened the first banking institution in Southern California around 1870. The following year, he reorganized the bank with several partners under the name Farmers and Merchants Bank.

Even more amazing was the fact that thirty-two-year-old John Downey was elected lieutenant governor in 1860. When Governor-Elect Milton S. Latham resigned his position to take a seat in the U.S. Senate a short time later, Downey became California's seventh governor. His wife, Maria Guirado Downey, was only twenty-one when she became first lady, the youngest woman to hold that title in California history.

During Downey's first year in office, the Civil War began. At that time, many Californians had Southern roots, thus backing the Confederacy. Downey didn't support Abraham Lincoln, and yet he obeyed the president's request to provide troops to serve the Union in California. Even though his decision to align California with Washington, DC, wasn't popular among many California residents, Downey believed in the preservation of the United States, contributing money and political support to the North throughout the war. That likely cost him reelection in 1862, as the bulk of the state's population was still loyal to the pro-slavery South. (See "Confederate Sympathizers in California," chapter 24.)

Despite this setback, Downey wasn't ruffled by his defeat. Returning to Los Angeles, he continued to make millions. In the 1870s, he turned his attention to bringing the Southern Pacific Railroad to Los Angeles. When Leland Stanford and his powerful business associates in Northern California announced their plans to build their railroad behind the Sierra Madre and San Gabriel Mountains, an angry Downey dug in his mighty heels. If Stanford and his associates had their way, the train line would bypass Los Angeles and the rest of the communities on the west side of the mountain range. The Southern Pacific's only rail line into the Southland would be a spur through the Cajon Pass to San Bernardino. Determined to change Stanford's mind, Downey and another leading Los Angeles businessman went to San Francisco to negotiate a deal with the owners of the Southern Pacific Railroad.

Although the Southern Pacific would need to be paid large concessions, the railroad tycoons accepted the offer, and work began. In September 1876, the new line was completed, forever linking Northern and Southern California. Of course, now rich and famous John Downey presided at the ceremony when the golden spike was driven into the rail line.

The Accident

Despite his immense success, Downey's marriage seemed to bring him his greatest joy. Maria and John didn't have any children, but the union was a happy one. His businesses required frequent trips, and despite their closeness, his wife often didn't travel with him.

Maria had a deathly fear of the very railroad that her husband had fought so hard to bring to Southern California. Most interesting is that Maria told John that she had a premonition about traveling on the train. And if she ever did, something terrible would happen to her. Of course, John reassured his nervous wife, talking her into taking the trip to San Francisco with him shortly after Christmas 1882 to visit friends for the holidays.

On their return trip on January 19, 1883, the weather turned foul. As usual, the southbound express train stopped at Tehachapi Summit to take on coal and water. It was three in the morning, and sleet and snow blew at gale force on the mountain pass. While the crew scrambled to finish the refueling process, John and Maria Downey slept in one of the two luxurious sleeper cars. The fact that the locomotive and tender were detached from the seven cars (sleepers, mail, express, baggage, coach, and smoker cars) remains a controversy. It's now generally accepted that at least two men uncoupled the cars with the intention of robbing the wealthy passengers on board.

The train station was built on a slight incline, so when the air brakes were released, the cars, still linked together, began to roll backward down the hill. The doomed coaches quickly picked up speed, barreling out of control four long miles. Reaching a sharp curve, the cars jumped the tracks and plummeted down the steep hillside into a canyon. The wooden coaches broke into pieces and caught fire, fueled by oil lamps and coal-burning stoves. Bodies of the dead and injured were strewn among the splintered debris along the cliffside and into the canyon below.

Dazed and severely injured, John awakened in terrible pain. Several uninjured passengers from the other cars pulled him through a broken window in the burning sleeping car. Sadly, Maria, the woman he loved dearly, the woman who had laid by his side minutes before the accident, was trapped in the tangle of burning debris. The rescuers tried desperately to save her, but the flames had been fanned by a gusting wind. The sleeping car was suddenly fully engulfed. Sadly, Maria Downey was burned alive. She was forty-six.

When her charred remains were finally recovered, she was mistaken for one of the other victims who had perished in the fire. After being shipped to a morgue in Los Angeles, she was misidentified by the coroner as Mrs. Cassell of San Francisco. Poor Maria was shipped to San Francisco, where she was finally correctly identified and, once again, taken back to Los Angeles.

Maria G. Downey was buried in the original Calvary Cemetery in Los Angeles. Another twist in the story is that when the old Calvary Cemetery was closed and the bodies dug up and reinterred in the cemetery's new location in East Los Angeles, Maria's body wasn't listed among the reburials. Were her remains left behind at the old cemetery's location where Cathedral High School was built in 1925? The records have been lost, and no one knows where Maria's final resting place is located.

The accounts of the final number of fatalities in the train accident differ, but between fifteen and twenty-one people, including former

Wisconsin congressman Charles H. Larrabee, died. Twelve others were severely injured.

Although John Downey recovered from his physical injuries, he never fully recovered emotionally. He lived another eleven years and married a woman named Rose Kelly. And yet, he was never the same man after the accident. Downey's life continued its downward slide. And when Rose died, Downey's emotional and physical health further declined.

John G. Downey died in April 1894. Though his life had been dedicated to his beloved Southern California, his body was shipped to San Francisco for burial. A large memorial to John Downey can be found in Holy Cross Catholic Cemetery in Colma, California.

John Downey's numerous other accomplishments include the following:

He formed a partnership with Phineas Banning to purchase 2,400 acres in San Pedro to lay out a city and harbor. Together, these two powerful men built a small railroad between the harbor and downtown Los Angeles. Shipping became easier, benefiting the business community of Los Angeles.

Downey helped organize the Los Angeles City Water Company to bring water into homes and buildings in the growing city.

He established the "Downey Block" in downtown Los Angeles, grouping businesses in his building—a sort of early mall system of shops. In fact, the Downey Block became the city's first true business center.

Together with two wealthy Angelenos, Downey donated 308 acres of prime land for the establishment of the University of Southern California in 1879. At that time, the land was valued at more than $1 million. Downey even served on the university's first board of trustees.

He was instrumental in opening the first public library in Los Angeles.

He established the Board of Trade (later called the Chamber of Commerce), serving as its first director.

Chapter 34
The Lucky Ladybug

IN THE DECADES FOLLOWING JOHN MARSHALL'S GOLD DISCOVERY IN 1848, tens of thousands of people poured into the new state of California. With so many mouths to feed in Northern California and very few ways to ship much-needed products to the West, agriculture became an important industry if the newly arrived people were to survive.

Shipments of beef were sent to Northern California from the ranchos in the southern portion of California. But in the 1860s, when a terrible drought nearly wiped out the cattle and sheep herds, many of the grand ranchos went bankrupt. Vast amounts of land were selling for pennies on the dollar, and the new entrepreneurs from Los Angeles and San Francisco gobbled up the available acreage.

When drought conditions had finally eased, former grazing land gave way to growing wheat, vineyards, citrus groves, and all sorts of vegetables. Enough crops were grown to take care of the needs of the burgeoning population throughout the state.

In the 1880s, agriculture production boomed when shipping perishable foods long distances became possible with the development of ice-cooled railroad cars. California farmers were then able to ship fresh fruit and vegetables outside of the state. One of the crops that grew exceptionally well in Southern California's soil and climate was oranges.

Neat rows of orange trees covered thousands of acres of once-barren landscape, and men became millionaires by growing the fragrant fruit. Because the booming orange industry provided jobs and bolstered the economy, oranges were called California's newfound "gold" and the state's latest "gold nugget."

Naturally, with millions of dollars riding on the success of the orange crops, the delicate groves were carefully guarded from blight, pests, and frosts. But when a tiny pest known as cotton scale arrived in a shipload of nursery stock from Australia in 1889, the valuable orange trees were ravaged. Cotton scale, a species of lice with an appetite for citrus plants, attacked the orchards with such voracity, it looked as if the orange industry was doomed.

In his book *Los Angeles, City of Dreams* (1935), author Harry Carr recalled seeing the invading pests when he was a child. He lived in a home situated in an orange grove and described the tiny bugs as having patches resembling soft cotton. He wrote that they had a red spot in the center that stained everything when it was squashed. The orange industry was "staggered to its knees," cutting down thousands of diseased and dying trees. The cost to the farmers and the state was devastating.

The Solution

Since the miniscule insects had come from "down under," the growers sent a representative to Australia hoping to find a native bug that fed on the cotton scale lice. The plan worked perfectly. A large colony of ladybugs survived the long ship voyage to California, and within a year, cotton scale was extinct.

As the savior of the "sacred tree of California," is it any wonder that the heroic ladybug is still associated with bringing good luck? Actually, the ladybug is considered a harbinger of good fortune in numerous countries, most likely for the same reason as they were revered in California—they kill destructive pests, like aphids, which devour plants and flowers. The myths of the little critters bringing good luck seem to be nearly universal. In Turkey, for example, they are simply called "the good luck bug." And in several cultures, their names contain religious connotations.

For decades, children have been taught that they should never harm a ladybug. If you're fortunate enough to have one land on you, make a wish and set it free. Never, never brush off a ladybug, for fear that you may do it harm. Instead, blow on it gently. And when it flies away, your wish will come true . . . not to mention the fact that, by letting the little creature go, it will continue to help the farmers' agricultural endeavors.

Chapter 35

A Royal Visitor in California

SUNDAY, DECEMBER 18, 1890: WITH A HUGE PUFF OF STEAM, THE PRI-
vate train that carried the king of Hawaii rolled to a stop in San Diego
Station, where the city's movers and shakers had gathered to welcome
him. King David Kalakaua was the first ruling monarch to visit the
United States. The king had included the San Diego area on his tour of
California at the request of John Spreckels, the region's richest and most
influential businessman, who was also a personal friend of the king's.

His Royal Highness emerged from his luxuriously outfitted car,
accompanied by several servants and official traveling companions.
Wearing his favorite straw hat—a regular fashion statement during the

King David Kalakaua of Hawaii (1882).

1890s—a dark frock coat, and white trousers, King Kalakaua was an impressive figure. His skin was deeply bronzed; his black, cropped hair was quite curly; and he had a thick mustache that melded into his even thicker, mutton-chop sideburns.

It wasn't often that someone of the king's stature visited San Diego, and newspaper reporters excitedly scribbled notes describing the event. No doubt John Spreckels and other city officials were delighted by the publicity the king's visit would bring to the area. After an exchange of greetings and a few speeches of welcome, the king and his party were whisked away to the Hotel del Coronado, where they would stay for the duration of His Majesty's visit.

It was already dark when the ferry crossed the bay. Looking back at San Diego, its gaslights glittering across the water, the king must have been reminded of his home in Honolulu. Later, he would comment about how much he liked San Diego, predicting that the city would have a "great future."

Even more dignitaries awaited the king and his entourage in Coronado. By now, it was nearly 11:00 p.m., and most of the area's residents were asleep. When the royal party reached the Hotel del Coronado, the king was escorted to his suite, Room 50. He needed rest, and lots of it. Kalakaua had been in poor health for quite some time. Although the king's true reason for visiting California was to rest and rejuvenate himself, reporters were told he made the journey to escape the political pressures in Hawaii. Ironically, if the king was trying to recover from the stresses that had weakened him both physically and mentally, his trip to California was a mistake that would cost him his life.

When he had arrived in San Francisco on December 4, Kalakaua's itinerary included parades, banquets, balls, and endless parties held in his honor. It was the same at each stop on his journey from Northern to Southern California. His days and nights had been filled with both social events and official obligations. The final leg of his trip to San Diego and the Hotel del Coronado was so that he could enjoy a warmer climate and have time to relax. And yet, once again, the king's social calendar quickly filled.

The first day after his arrival, King Kalakaua hosted a reception for the officers of the army and navy in the hotel's beautiful parlors. Immediately after that affair ended, he attended a second, less formal reception for the people of Coronado Island. Hundreds of local citizens lined up to meet the hotel's famous guest. One can only imagine the Victorian ladies attempting to curtsey before the monarch. Dressed in his stately uniform, complete with gold epaulets and knee-high leather boots, the king must have looked quite handsome and amazingly civilized, considering most people of that era thought Hawaii was a land filled with half-naked "savages."

Instead, the Americans who met David Kalakaua soon discovered he was an eloquent speaker, as well as an accomplished musician, writer, and politician. He had received his education in Hawaii's finest schools, read voraciously, and had taken a trip around the world in 1874, the first king to have ever done so. At his palace in Honolulu, he had surrounded himself with writers, poets, and artists. Kalakaua had even written the country's melodious national anthem, "Hawaii Ponoi."

Born in Honolulu in 1836, David Kalakaua was the descendant of high-ranking Hawaiian chiefs. He had been elected to the throne by the Hawaiian parliament in 1874, ruling during a time of great prosperity in the Islands. Ironically, it was that same economic success that would eventually cause the downfall of the Hawaiian monarchy. But for the time being, the Hawaiian treasury overflowed with tax money paid by the affluent sugar plantations and other non-Hawaiian businessmen living in the Islands. As the non-Hawaiians had gained more prominence and power, however, they became increasingly critical of Kalakaua's extravagant spending habits. The king's lavish parties were famous, and the local newspapers had a field day with stories about the supposed "drunken orgies" held at the king's boathouse located on Honolulu Harbor. In reality, the so-called orgies were nothing more than small private parties, or luaus, held by His Majesty. It was at these luaus, which were often attended by foreign dignitaries and famous visitors like Robert Louis Stevenson, where Kalakaua escaped the pressures of his position.

The Hawaiian people loved King Kalakaua. He had reinstated the hula, once banished by the American missionaries who had brought Christianity to the Islands. Kalakaua often entertained his boathouse guests with both male and female dancers, who performed the ancient dances and chants. Much to the horror of Honolulu's elite non-Hawaiian society, the women dancers wore only a lei of flowers around their necks to cover their breasts. Reportedly, many haole (white) businessmen attended Kalakaua's boathouse parties, though it's doubtful they told their wives!

THE SPRECKELS CONNECTION

For decades, Kalakaua had struggled to maintain control of his little kingdom in the Pacific. Shortly after he had become king, he allied himself closely with Claus Spreckels, the powerful sugar magnate from California. The king gave Spreckels financial advantages over the other plantation owners. In return, Kalakaua received "favors" from Spreckels. Obviously understanding Hawaii's potential to make him even richer, Spreckels created a huge sugar plantation on Maui. His son, John D., soon became a partner in the Maui project. Both Spreckels were more than mere business associates with the king of Hawaii. While John spent most of his time at his home in San Francisco prior to his move to San Diego after the 1906 earthquake, Claus had lived in the Islands off and on for years. In fact, he was known as the king's "poker-playing" buddy, frequently attending the infamous parties at the royal boathouse.

By the late 1880s, the king had begun to lose power over his monarchy. Yet, he and the Spreckelses remained friends. On his last visit to California, Kalakaua stayed at Claus's ranch in Aptos on Monterey Bay for five days. And when the king arrived at the Hotel del Coronado, John D. was there, too. In fact, John Spreckels provided a Hawaiian flag to hoist from the hotel's roof. During the king's stay, the two men would spend a great deal of time together.

Like his other stopovers, Kalakaua's San Diego visit was a frenzy of parties and sightseeing trips. Great crowds gathered wherever he went. When he was taken on a horseback ride through downtown San Diego, the streets were filled with well-wishers. There were speeches, followed by meetings, operas, dinners, and public and private receptions. One day, Kalakaua was taken to see Sweetwater reservoir, then considered Southern California's most amazing engineering feat. He continued on to National City for another reception for about one hundred residents. Finally, the royal party crossed the Mexican border, where the king met with government officials and smoked Mexican cigarettes "with great relish."

With his grueling schedule, is it any wonder that the king had become so weak that his visit to San Diego had to be cut short? Of course, there was no public mention of his failing health and exhaustion. Instead, he said he needed to return home, as there were growing political complications in Hawaii.

When King Kalakaua reached Santa Barbara, he forced himself to attend more social events. It was then that he suffered a mild stroke and lapsed into a coma. A doctor accompanied the king on the journey to San Francisco. But it was useless. Despite the doctors' best efforts, King David Kalakaua died on January 20 at the age of fifty-four. His old friend, Claus Spreckels, was by his side when he died. Though the official cause of death was ruled "Bright's disease," most Hawaiians still believe that their king died of a broken heart, knowing that his kingdom would eventually be lost to the United States.

When they received the news about the king's death, the people of San Diego speculated that it was the cold that the king caught at the Masonic Lodge that "finished him." Folks said that Kalakaua had made a mistake when he sat beside an open window, and that it had been a chilly night. Apparently, he never fully recovered from the cold. Coupled with his whirlwind visit to the Golden State, it had all been more than his fragile body could take.

On January 22, there was a huge memorial service held for the king in San Francisco. Later that day, the casket, draped with the Hawaiian flag, was placed aboard a ship bound for Hawaii. The ship's hull and spars were draped with black, its flags flying at half-mast. As the ship carrying the king's body left the wharf, the USS *Charleston* fired its minute guns to salute the fallen king. Large crowds had gathered around the bay to watch the ship make its way through the Golden Gate and, finally, to disappear into the sunset.

This occurred before the telegraph lines had been laid across the Pacific. Sadly, the Hawaiian people wouldn't know about the king's passing until the flagship arrived in Honolulu Harbor a week later. Although the king's sister, Liliuokalani, would take over the throne, David Kalakaua's death was the beginning of the end of the Hawaiian monarchy.

Chapter 36

Margaret Eaton and Santa Cruz Island

SANTA CRUZ ISLAND GOT ITS NAME FROM AN UNUSUAL INCIDENT THAT occurred in 1769, when the first Spaniards visited the island. An estimated two thousand Chumash Indians ("Lumi" in the Chumash language) lived on the island at that time. They were skilled fishermen who braved the choppy channel waters to trade with tribes on the mainland. The Chumash greeted the strange, fair-skinned men with open arms. Leading the newcomers to a village near what is now called Prisoner's Bay, the Spaniards were given gifts of fish and fresh water. In return,

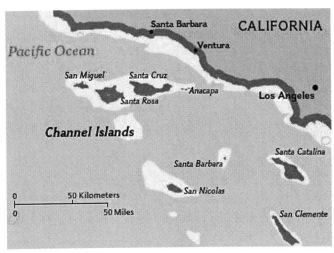

Map of California's Channel Islands (2007).

the Spanish presented the Indigenous people with glass beads to show their appreciation. Franciscan priests always accompanied the soldiers and explorers on these early expeditions in California with the hope of "converting the heathens." This trip was no exception.

As night fell, the Spanish entourage made its way back to the ship. Suddenly, the priest realized he had left his staff in the village. Believing the Natives wouldn't return the holy object, the priest assumed his staff was lost forever. Much to the Spaniards' surprise, a small canoe approached the ship at the crack of dawn. One of the Indigenous men had found the staff with the "holy cross" on top. After climbing onboard, he presented it to the overjoyed priest. Because of this act of honesty, the Franciscan named the island Isla de Santa Cruz, or "Island of the Holy Cross."

When the Spanish settled Alta California, the Chumash were allowed to stay on Santa Cruz. By 1814, a measles epidemic had already decimated the tribe, and those who survived were removed to Santa Barbara.

As the decades passed, Santa Cruz was sold and resold to individuals who opted to use the island for sheep ranching. Eventually, Justinian Caire, a wealthy businessman from San Francisco, took over the operation. He and his family moved to Santa Cruz Island, expanding the sheep-ranching enterprise and constructing additional buildings, including ranch and bunk houses, barns, wineries, a blacksmith shop, and a chapel.

While Caire was building his ranching empire in the inner portions of the island, the beautiful bays and coves drew campers, fishermen, and seal hunters to the rugged coastline. One of these fishermen was Ira Eaton, a young man with a small fishing boat and a big dream. Ira saw the potential for tourism on Santa Cruz and hoped he would find a way to set up a permanent camp, a place where he could bring tourists from the mainland to hunt, fish, and enjoy ocean activities, just like Catalina Island's ever-popular Avalon Bay.

MARGARET HOLDEN EATON

Margaret Holden was born in Quebec, Canada, in 1876, and her father was the captain of a tugboat on the St. Lawrence River. Her mother died when she was five, and she and her baby brother were sent to a convent for a number of years. Margaret was educated and had even attended a private academy for girls. After she was finished with school, she had no intention of settling down. She worked odd jobs, saved her money, and waited for an opportunity to present itself.

When Margaret was seventeen, her father died. Devastated by his death, she longed to leave Canada and move somewhere new. The opportunity she had been hoping for happened when several of her girlfriends invited her to move to San Diego, California, with them. They were all taking waitressing jobs at the fabulous Hotel del Coronado on a beautiful stretch of beach. Margaret jumped at the chance to go.

In her biography, Margaret wrote about spending her days on the beach in front of the hotel. Sun, sand, and surf were her new loves. When her employer sent her to work at a new luxurious hotel in Arizona, she said she longed to feel the cool ocean breezes on her face again. It wasn't the desert that called to her, but the sea.

In 1902, she got her wish. She was hired to work at the first-class Potter Hotel in Santa Barbara, where California's rich and famous often stayed. She waited on guests like John D. Rockefeller and his family on numerous occasions. Life was filled with fun moments: parties, time at the beach, and long walks to the old mission or through town with friends. She met her future husband, Ira Eaton, one evening on a hayride.

After a short courtship, the pair was married, making their home in Santa Barbara. Ira caught sea lions for circuses and zoos, laid out traps to catch crawfish (lobster), and netted mackerel to sell at the fish markets in Santa Barbara. It was a dangerous job that kept him away from home for weeks at a time.

Margaret gave birth to a baby girl named Vera. More than ever, she missed Ira's companionship. But Ira refused to give up the sea and get a job on the mainland. Instead, around 1909, he suggested his wife and baby move to Santa Cruz Island, where he could come ashore at the end of the day to see them. Most women would have balked at living on an island hours away by boat from the nearest town. Love must have clouded Margaret's judgment, for life on the desolate island not only meant spending her days alone, but she would have to fend for herself and Vera most of the time. They lived in a dirt-floored shanty, cooked on a camp stove, and hauled water and wood from a nearby canyon. The ocean was always cold, but that's where Margaret and Vera had to bathe. And when other water sources dried up in the summer months, she stood knee-deep in the sea to wash everything from pans and dishes to their clothes and bedding.

Margaret not only succeeded at these challenges but also excelled at adapting to the barebones lifestyle she and her husband chose to live. After a few years of camping in various locations, the Eatons finally received permission to build a tourist camp at Pelican Bay.

Their efforts paid off, for word about their camp soon spread. In fact, it became so popular that guests often booked a year in advance. The rich and famous of the 1920s and 1930s sailed to the Eatons' camp. Arriving in their expensive yachts, they anchored in the bay, coming ashore to enjoy "Mother" Eaton's wonderful cooking. Other tourists stayed in the little cabins Ira had constructed. There was no electricity, no running water, and no indoor toilets. Perhaps their most famous visitor was actor John Barrymore, who frequently returned to what he said was one of his favorite places on earth.

Numerous "Hollywood people," including Gloria Swanson, Jesse Lasky, and Cecil B. DeMille, stayed at the Eatons' camp while filming movies. Santa Cruz Island's beautiful coastline frequently doubled for a South Seas location, though barges of palm and coconut trees had to be hauled in to lend an air of authenticity.

Mother Eaton's hospitality and good cooking became somewhat legendary. Margaret was quite skilled at making tasty dishes from local plants, animals, and seafood. Among the favorite fare was wild boar, roasted Hawaiian style in a pit with lots of garlic; fluffy biscuits with cactus jam; fried potatoes; and fresh vegetables from her garden. There were always cakes and pies served for dessert.

As Margaret aged, she never lost her spunk. Her book, titled *Sea Captain's Wife*, is filled with adventurous stories about violent storms that flooded the camp. Trees were washed away. Boulders tumbled so close to the shanty that Margaret thought she and little Vera would surely die. One of her most frightening experiences was when she and Vera were attacked by a group of bandits. Margaret fought them off with a knife, then snatched up the child and ran to her rowboat. The crooks fired shots at the mother and child, though neither was hit. Luckily, a Portuguese fishing boat was nearby and rescued them. While they headed into Santa Barbara to report the incident, a thick fog rolled in. As if Margaret and Vera hadn't had enough excitement, the fishing boat was nearly rammed by a huge lumber schooner.

Nothing seemed to faze this courageous woman. Despite the hardships and dangers of living on Santa Cruz, Margaret and Vera returned to the camp at Pelican Bay. Even when Vera left to attend public school in Santa Barbara, Margaret and Ira stayed on their beloved island.

Things suddenly changed in 1937 when the Eatons received word they had to immediately vacate Santa Cruz. In her book, Margaret wrote that the news came as a shock. Apparently, the island was sold to a new owner who wouldn't allow them to continue operating their camp at Pelican Bay. At the age of sixty-one, Margaret left Santa Cruz Island. It was the last time she would ever see the place she had spent most of her life.

Unlike most of the other Channel Islands, Santa Cruz has natural springs. Streams gather force as they flow from the mountain ranges into the deep valleys. Here and there, rivers cascade over canyon walls in ribboned waterfalls. Needless to say, Santa Cruz Island's natural beauty has attracted generations of artists, photographers, and nature lovers to its shores.

Amazing Santa Cruz Island is no longer in private hands. The Nature Conservancy owns and manages the western 76 percent of the island, while the eastern 24 percent is owned and managed by the National Park Service. There's only one way to get to Santa Cruz Island—by boat. For those of us who don't own yachts, the official concessionaire is Island Packers Cruises, which offers sightseeing trips to Santa Cruz, Anacapa, San Miguel, and Santa Barbara Islands.

THE TWENTIETH CENTURY DAWNS

Chapter 37

Chicken of the Sea

IT'S HARD TO IMAGINE A TIME WHEN AMERICANS DIDN'T EAT TUNA sandwiches, or when the ever-popular tuna casserole didn't grace the tables at church potlucks. Surprisingly, canned tuna has only been around for a little over one hundred years. Its discovery was the result of an act of nature that nearly bankrupted a fish cannery. And it all happened right here in California.

The story of the tuna industry began around 1900 when Alfred P. Halfhill, owner of a sardine canning factory in San Francisco, moved his business to San Pedro. Halfhill had heard that Southern California's ocean waters teamed with all kinds of fish and that sardines numbered in the tens of millions.

Since the late 1800s, fish canneries in San Francisco and Monterey had been an important part of California's burgeoning economy. But up to that point, no one had tapped into the potential fishery market in Southern California. Halfhill was the first of many who had the foresight to establish a fish canning business in the southern half of the state, a decision that would ultimately earn him a fortune.

Appropriately named the Southern California Fish Company, Half-hill's new business operated swimmingly well for its first few years. But in 1903, something strange happened—the sardines suddenly disappeared. While today's scientists understand that the sardine population ebbs and flows about every sixty years, fishermen in the past had no idea what happened to the millions of silvery little swimmers.

With the company facing ruin, Mr. Halfhill's staff scrambled to find a substitute to fill thousands of empty cans. Although the sardines had vanished, there were still plenty of other fish in the sea. A large fish known as "tunny," or tuna, was quite abundant between the mainland and the Channel Islands. But how would these albacore tuna taste when cooked and canned? If only the company could find the right formula for processing the fish, then tuna would be the perfect solution to the company's problem. After various recipes were tested, the formula was set, and the canned tuna industry was born.

Unfortunately, the public's reception was less than enthusiastic, and the Southern California Fish Company was stuck with seven hundred cases of unsold tuna. A new marketing strategy had to be found.

Because raw tuna fish turns white when heated, the cannery's foreman, Wilbur Wood, came up with an idea that was nothing less than brilliant. They would promote tuna fish as "chicken of the sea." (Many years later, this would become the registered trademark of another tuna cannery.) After all, if consumers associated tuna with the familiar and popular poultry, they might find their canned tuna fish more palatable. The cannery made a deal with a coffee company so that anyone buying their product received a free can of tuna with their purchase. The plan worked perfectly, and as the years passed, Americans acquired a taste for tuna. It was a relatively cheap protein source that could be used in a variety of recipes. By World War II, Mr. Halfhill's prediction that canned tuna would eventually be found in nearly every American pantry had finally come true.

Although Southern California's tuna industry thrived for decades, overfished waters off the California coast forced the canneries to move to other coastal locations. But because of Halfhill's success at marketing tuna, by the time of his death in 1924, there were thirty-six canneries processing canned tuna on the West Coast.

And does tuna really taste like chicken? Not really. But for millions of people who love it, they're quite happy with the flavor and convenience of merely opening a can for a high-protein, low-calorie meal.

Chapter 38
The Murder of Jane Stanford

WHILE MOST AMERICANS HAVE HEARD OF LELAND STANFORD, FOUNDER of Stanford University, few people know that his wife, Jane, was murdered. Although there have been many theories through the years, to this day the mystery of who poisoned her and why remains unsolved.

Our story begins with Mr. Stanford's rise to power and his unbelievable wealth. Old California had many successful men who came to the state seeking gold. Most who became rich, however, made their

Photo of Leland and Jane
Stanford (ca. 1850).

fortunes by taking gold from the men who did the backbreaking physical labor. Stanford fell into the latter category, selling merchandise at highly inflated prices. He wasn't born into poverty like so many of his San Francisco millionaire peers. He was highly educated and earned his law degree in New York in 1845.

Stanford had been practicing law for a few years in Milwaukee, Wisconsin, when his well-to-do father presented him with his own law library. Stanford served as the county's district attorney and became one of the area's most successful lawyers. It was during this time Leland Stanford met Jane Elizabeth Lathrop, the daughter of a New York merchant, marrying her in 1850. For the next two years, life was good for the Stanfords until, in a twist of fate, Stanford lost nearly everything when his law library and other properties were burned in a devastating fire.

Of course, by then news about California's gold had swept around the world, and the goldfields were crawling with prospectors in need of supplies. Leland joined his five brothers in California, where they opened a general store in Michigan Bluff, a town in Placer County close to where their potential customers lived and mined. He also used his expertise as a lawyer, serving as the region's justice of the peace. As Leland Stanford's profits soared, he bought up mining interests, property, and even a busy saloon.

But the mining camps in the mountains were too rough for Jane, who had temporarily moved back to her home in Albany, New York. When Leland built a beautiful home for her in Sacramento, Jane finally moved to California in 1856. From there, everything Stanford touched seemed to turn to gold. Besides his numerous business successes, he served as the state's governor from 1862 to 1863 during the Civil War.

Over the ensuing years, Leland Stanford was involved in establishing everything from library systems to banks to life insurance companies. His most well-known contribution to California's history occurred in 1868, when he teamed up with three of Northern California's most successful businessmen: Collis Huntington, Mark Hopkins, and Charles Crocker. Collectively, they were known as "The Associates" or "The Big Four."

Responsible for bringing the Central Pacific Railroad to the northern part of the state, they were an unstoppable team. Stanford was elected president of the new railroad, and in his honor, the first steam engine was named *Gov. Stanford*. Stanford officiated at the ceremony in Utah when the "Golden Spike" was pounded into tracks that united the east and west coasts of America. Following the success of the Union Pacific, the Big Four worked to connect the entire state, establishing the Southern Pacific Railroad and laying tracks from Northern to Southern California.

Meanwhile, Mrs. Stanford had become one of Northern California's most sought-after women at social events and charitable functions. But Jane's main focus was her son, Leland Stanford Jr. The Stanfords had tried to have children for nearly eighteen years. Jane finally became pregnant at the age of thirty-nine, considered well past the safest time for a woman to give birth. Several contemporary newspaper articles reported that young Leland was constantly in poor health. Yet, he was an extremely intelligent boy on track to attend Harvard. He had a keen interest in archaeology and collecting artifacts, a result of the endless trips to foreign countries as a part of what his parents felt was an important part of his education. It was on one of these extended times overseas that fifteen-year-old Leland Jr. became extremely ill with typhoid fever. His parents brought him to Florence, Italy, believing the Tuscan climate would benefit his health. Sadly, the boy died.

Mr. and Mrs. Stanford were crushed by his loss. Exhausted, Stanford claimed that when he laid down to rest a few days after his son's death, he had a dream—a dream in which Leland Jr. gave him a message. According to Stanford, his son told him to "not give up" and to "live for humanity." Whether Mr. Stanford had imagined the strange encounter, or if his son had really returned to help him, Leland Jr.'s words deeply affected Stanford's life. He later declared that since he had lost his own child, all the children of California would now be his children. He and Jane would build a wonderful university on their vast Palo Alto property, finding the best teachers and staff to help them run it. And thus, after spending an estimated $154,000,000 to establish Leland Stanford Junior University, it was finally opened in 1885.

Jane and Leland had had their fingers in virtually every decision made concerning the buildings, grounds, and staffing. They sat on the Board of Directors and made sure things were operating to their satisfaction.

As if Stanford hadn't accomplished enough, he was elected to the U.S. Senate in 1885, serving in that position until his death in 1893. As difficult as his loss was for Jane, she continued her involvement in the university's affairs. But it soon became obvious that not everyone liked her "interference."

After her husband's death, Jane Stanford, the woman of means who had worn layers of diamond bracelets on her wrists and strands of priceless pearls that hung to her waist, was suddenly without liquid cash. Most surprising was that Mr. Stanford's estate was tied up in probate litigation for years. In the meantime, there were ongoing expenses to be paid. Jane was determined to keep their beloved university afloat and resorted to terminating much of her staff and selling off her jewelry—anything to keep the university running. She was remarkable, strong, and she continued her work with Stanford University until the end of her life.

The Murder

Who poisoned Jane Stanford? It happened not once, but twice. The first time, it occurred in her own home, an enormous San Francisco mansion on Nob Hill. On Saturday, January 14, 1905, a number of people had come and gone during the day, and a few had stayed for dinner. Of course, the Stanfords' staff was present. It was Jane's usual habit to drink bottled Poland Mineral Spring Water before bed each night. After drinking a portion of the water, she began to feel sick. Calling for help from her maid, she was forced to vomit repeatedly, writhing in pain on the floor. The doctor was called, and based on her symptoms, he believed she had been poisoned.

The remaining water was tested for various poisons. The laboratory found the culprit was a high dose of rat poison and strychnine, and that her life was likely saved by her maid, who had forced warm water into her stomach to make her vomit until her stomach was empty. Naturally, a woman of Jane Stanford's reputation and stature required a police investigation to determine who had tried to kill her.

Anyone and everyone who had been in the house that day was a suspect. Who had access to the bottled Poland Mineral Spring Water stored in the back kitchen? And why would anyone want to harm her? And what possible motive was there for doing away with her? After the obvious suspects like the household staff had been questioned and released, the unsolved case was turned over to the Henry Morse Detective Agency, San Francisco's famous team of sleuths rivaling Pinkerton's detectives.

While the case floundered without any resolution or reason for the heinous crime, Jane's doctor recommended that she rest somewhere warm and far away from San Francisco to recuperate from the trauma. A month later, on February 15, Jane and her entourage of maids and trusted staff sailed on the SS *Alameda* to Honolulu, Hawaii. She checked into the beautiful Moana Hotel on the beach in Waikiki, enjoying the gentle breezes and beautiful ocean view.

On February 28, Jane Stanford felt much better and accepted the invitation to enjoy a carriage ride to the other side of the Pali where she and her assistant, Miss Berner, and a few friends had a lovely picnic. In the late afternoon, they returned to the Moana and had a light dinner on the veranda. Miss Berner later testified Mrs. Stanford had eaten too many chocolates with her lunch, implying Jane had indigestion that evening. Whether or not it was the case, she asked the maid for a glass of bicarbonate of soda to calm her sensitive stomach. Mrs. Stanford had brought a bottle of her favorite bicarbonate powder from home. Until that night, however, she hadn't needed it.

Within two hours, the poor woman could be heard screaming for help from inside her suite. When Miss Berner entered, she found Jane on the floor, her body morphed into a cramped and agonized position. And once again, her maid tried to get her to vomit by forcing her to drink warm water. This time, however, her muscles were in such spasm, her jaw was unable to be opened. Nothing could be done to help her. The hotel's doctor had brought a stomach pump to her room, but Jane was now beyond help. Her last words had been that she knew she had been poisoned again . . . and this time, she knew she was going to die.

When Mrs. Stanford's maid told the hotel doctor what had happened in San Francisco, he immediately opened the suspect bottle of bicarbonate powder, dipped in his finger, and took a tiny taste. It was so bitter; he intuitively knew it contained a high level of strychnine.

An autopsy conducted by officials in Hawaii determined Jane Stanford had indeed been poisoned and that the bicarbonate of soda had contained the poison.

Before Jane's body had been returned to California for burial, Dr. Jordan, president of Stanford University, arrived in Honolulu. He hired his own doctor and had him declare Mrs. Stanford had died of heart failure. Releasing the story to the newspapers, Jordan insisted there had been no poisoning. Thus, the findings of the Hawaiian police, doctors, and the verdict of murder by the Hawaiian coroner's jury were completely ignored.

Why would the university's president get involved in the murder investigation? And why would he do everything in his power to cover up the crime? It seems as if his first thought was that he needed to hush up what would have been a huge problem for the school. As a result of Dr. Jordan's interference, the culprit or culprits who put the poison in the Poland Water and the bottle of bicarbonate were never found and prosecuted.

In fact, it wasn't until the case was later reexamined by Dr. Robert Cutler, a professor at Stanford University, and several other authorities that it was determined Dr. Jordan had indeed perpetrated a coverup to protect the reputation of the university. In his book *The Mysterious Death of Jane Stanford*, Dr. Cutler goes into minute detail regarding the investigations and concealment of the truth for the crime committed 115 years earlier.

And yet, to this day, the case is unsolved. Everyone involved has died, and all that investigators have left to work with are the documents that simply buried the evidence. And sadly, we'll likely never know who was behind the murder of Jane Lathrop Stanford, the "Mother of Leland Stanford Junior University."

Chapter 39

The Fabulous Palace Hotel

BY 1875, SAN FRANCISCO WAS IN THE THROES OF SHAKING OFF ITS frontier dust and showing the world it had become a "modern" city. The bay was the biggest and best port on the West Coast. The steady stream of prospectors arriving in San Francisco had begun to slow, as land claims were gobbled up by private mining companies. It was the merchants who been the real winners in the gold rush of 1849. Businesses that had started in canvas tents were now housed in proper brick buildings. Banks and bathhouses, hotels, theaters, and restaurants had sprouted up like mushrooms along the waterfront, now stretching back from the wharfs

Photo of the "World's Finest Hotel" before the 1906 earth-quake and fire.

into the hills. Union Square, the center of town, was a miniature metropolis, a mere foreshadowing of what was yet to come.

It was against this backdrop of prosperity and growth that two men of great vision, Senator William Sharon (see "The Deadly Sharon Scandal," chapter 30) and banker William Chapman Ralston, undertook building a grand hotel in 1875 unlike anything the world had seen up to this point.

Aptly named "The Palace," the magnificent structure covered an entire block, towered seven stories high, and "featured four hydraulic elevators known as 'rising rooms' in which guests could reach the hotel's loftiest heights in comfort and style." Rooms were equipped with an electric call button, a unique concept in an era that hadn't yet seen room service.

Ultimately, the world's largest and finest hotel would cost more than $5 million to build, an unimaginable figure in those days. Sadly, Mr. Ralston's grand dream had become his undoing. His bank was drained of cash, and it would soon be forced to close its doors. Rather than facing what lay ahead, he ended his own life mere weeks before the Palace's grand opening.

Ralston's partner, Senator Sharon, saw to it that the Palace became history's most luxurious hotel. As word about the beautiful structure

Photo of the burning Palace Hotel. Only the outer shell remained (1906).

spread around the globe, kings, princes, and presidents became frequent visitors. For the next three decades, the grand hotel prospered.

And then the unthinkable happened. In the early morning hours of April 18, 1906, the low growl that rumbled through the area was followed by violent shaking. Though the earthquake lasted only a minute, the city had been mortally wounded. An estimated six thousand people were killed. Countless others were injured or trapped in the rubble. Aftershocks would bring down even more buildings.

Although the Palace Hotel had experienced structural damage, it had stood its ground. Guests had been thrown from their beds, including Enrico Caruso, who fled his room wearing only a towel. Legend has it that the famous tenor later told reporters he would never return to San Francisco . . . not that there would have been much for him to return to for quite some time. In any case, he lived up to his promise.

While some survivors fled the city, others did their best to rescue those trapped in the debris. Fires from leaking gas mains had erupted all over the city, quickly spreading from structure to structure. In the ensuing hours, flames crept closer to the magnificent hotel. Because the water mains had been broken as the earth had been twisted and jarred, the fire department was almost helpless. Given the magnitude of the tragedy and the limited manpower, there was nothing much anyone could do to stop the advancing flames.

After three excruciating days, the fire finally burned itself out. More than twenty-five thousand buildings, including the Palace Hotel, had been swallowed up in the firestorm. Gone were the original art treasures adorning its walls, the imported antique furnishings, and the expensive draperies and carpets. All that remained were a few outside walls.

Three years later in 1909, the rebuilt Palace Hotel opened its doors, this time at a staggering cost of $10 million. Though the new hotel was even grander, the architects made sure the structure included many of the original hotel's famous features.

Perhaps the most spectacular portion of the remodeled Palace Hotel was the Garden Court (formerly called the "Grand Court"). Originally, the area served as the hotel's carriage entrance. Odors from the horses (and, later, auto emissions) drifted into the hotel and annoyed the guests

. . . an unsuitable situation for the world's most lavish hotel. It's not surprising the carriage entrance was closed and replaced with what has been called one of the most beautiful places anywhere. The Garden Court is the hotel's main dining room and banquet hall. Crowned by a spectacular $7 million stained-glass dome, the Garden Court is adorned by a double row of massive Italian marble columns and Austrian crystal chandeliers.

Today, the historic Palace Hotel is considered one of the world's Grande Dame hotels. Honored by such prestigious organizations as the National Trust for Historic Preservation and the American Institute of Architects, the landmark hotel continues to attract the world's rich and famous to its elegant doors.

Some Important (and Not So Important) Events

1876   The emperor of Brazil tells San Francisco's mayor, "Nothing makes me ashamed of Brazil so much as the Palace Hotel."

1887   Actress Sarah Bernhardt checks into the hotel with her baby tiger.

1919   President Woodrow Wilson hosts two luncheons to gather support for the signing of the Versailles Treaty that ended World War I.

1920s   The hotel's master chef creates Green Goddess salad dressing. The delicious sauce is named in honor of an English actor, who stayed there while performing in a play called *The Green Goddess*.

1945   The United Nations holds a banquet in the elegant Garden Court to honor its opening session.

1980s   The hotel receives landmark status.

Rescued from the flames, the hotel's gold cutlery is reportedly one of the oldest gold dinner services in the world. It has been used at dinners for important guests, like Prince Philip, Duke of Edinburgh; President William McKinley; and General Ulysses S. Grant.

One of the Palace's original murals was painted by Maxfield Parrish. The celebrated *Pied Piper of Hamelin* graces the wall in the Pied Piper Bar, which has been proclaimed as "One of the World's Seven Greatest Bars" by *Esquire Magazine*.

Chapter 40

The School of Artistic Whistling

ONCE UPON A TIME, LONG BEFORE THE DAYS OF CDS AND DOWNLOADED digital music, most people whistled to entertain themselves. Experts on all things whistling tell us that the "art" began with our primitive ancestors. Who can say when the first human rounded his or her lips, took a breath, and let out the unique sound to signal their tribe? Whistles carry farther than most people's voices and can be disguised to mimic birds, thus avoiding detection by the enemy.

Whistling as musical entertainment dates back centuries—to the Renaissance and likely even earlier. Man-made instruments were still primitive by today's standards, and the human whistle was substituted for the high notes now made by piccolos or flutes. This type of whistling was called *Kunstpfeifen* (literally, art-whistling). As wind instruments were perfected and their pitch became more reliable, fewer and fewer whistlers were used in formal orchestras. Art-whistling continued as a form of entertainment in private homes and smaller venues well into the nineteenth century.

Performance whistling became popular again during the years of vaudeville (ca. 1840–1940), but it wasn't the kind of whistling that would have been done with an orchestra. Vaudeville appealed to the masses, and *Kunstpfeifen* whistling to accompany the classical music of Mozart or Vivaldi had no place at the corner theater, where audiences expected to be entertained with acrobats, comical acts, and song-and-dance routines. A new kind of whistling became popular. A typical vaudeville whistler performed folk and show tunes, not trying to sound like an instrument, but using the sounds from his puckered lips to make a tune. He might be accompanied by a small band or simply a piano, but the whistle substituted for a voice.

With the popularity of whistling, bird sounds were added for variety. Some entertainers simply imitated bird calls, while others incorporated chirps and warbles here and there into the tune. Bird-influenced whistling became so fashionable that Agnes Woodward, a whistling afficionado, opened a school of whistling in Los Angeles, California, in 1909.

Agnes studied voice at Detroit's Conservatory of Music. We'll never know why the accomplished singer became attracted to whistling, but the fact is that she began an in-depth study of the "art" while still in college. Whistling wasn't merely a pastime or entertainment. It was her passion, her life's work.

Moving to Los Angeles in 1902, young Agnes earned her living by giving private whistling lessons. When she founded the Agnes Woodward California School of Artistic Whistling seven years later, she trained her students in whistling techniques, including what she called the "bird method." Agnes had become particularly intrigued with the variety of sounds birds make and began to experiment with imitating the nuances of nature's own whistlers. Graduates went on to have successful careers in vaudeville, and for decades, the school's whistling quartets and its large chorus performed at events around the Southland.

And what, you may be thinking, would a student learn at a whistling school? First, Agnes standardized a series of bird-inspired whistling sounds. She analyzed the patterns of sounds for various birds, breaking them down into categories, such as trills, flutters, and warbles. Students learned not only how to read and write music but also how to use the symbols for bird sounds in musical scores.

And then there are the techniques: "*Sporgendo*" is the traditional mode, with rounded or puckered lips, while "palatal" whistling is produced by placing the tongue against the roof of the mouth. Let's not forget "finger whistling," and its many forms, including *yubibue*, which is popular in Japan, and *fortissimo*, used for calling a cab.

There's also a method to breathing while whistling a tune. Circular breathing is a technique that allows a performer to whistle an entire tune without an obvious breath. A variety of techniques are used to produce special musical effects, like *legato* and multiphonics (a special technique where several notes are produced at the same time).

Agnes Woodward's school remained open until 1945, when vaudeville was replaced by movies and whistling's popularity was replaced by the Big Band sound.

As if you don't already know more about whistling than you ever cared to, here are a few fascinating facts:

- The human whistle is considered a part of the flute family.
- Whistlers once performed in operas.
- By the turn of the twentieth century, whistling music was an accepted part of the music industry.
- Throughout history, and in many parts of the world, whistling was associated with the occult. Whistling in ancient Greece was taboo.
- Whistling annoys many people because of its high-pitched timbre (sine wave), which is similar to the tone of an old-fashioned cash register. Roughly 1 percent of the population is affected negatively by hearing the sound of whistling.
- There's still an International Artwhistling Philharmonic Society, and they're very serious about this musical form.

The International Whistlers' Convention is held annually during the third or fourth week of April. It takes place in Louisburg, North Carolina, which is the official "Whistling Capital of the World." Besides the whistling contests, there are concerts and other musical events featuring the world's best whistlers. In churches throughout the area, hymns are whistled, rather than sung . . . which would have been considered sacrilege a few hundred years ago.

In 1986, the International Whistlers Convention established its Hall of Fame Award to honor people who have made great contributions to the art of whistling. Agnes Woodward was the first recipient.

Chapter 41

Surfing Comes to California

CENTURIES AGO, THE SPORT OF SURFING WAS BORN UPON HAWAII'S TUR-
quoise breakers. Once a pastime enjoyed by Hawaiian royalty, it was nearly
snuffed out by puritanical New England missionaries who arrived on the
Islands in the early 1800s. Over the ensuing decades, the well-meaning
missionaries did their best to obliterate the Hawaiian culture. When it
came to surfboard riding, they considered it a frivolous waste of time and
the scanty bathing attire indecent.

Photo of George Freeth.

Ironically, by the end of the nineteenth century many grandsons of the very missionaries who had tried to ban the sport were among the Islands' best surfers. They rode the breakers at the ever-popular Waikiki Beach, shoulder to shoulder with the Hawaiians whose ancestors had created the leisure activity.

The true revival of surfboard riding began in Hawaii around 1900 when a young Hawaiian named George Freeth created a thinner, lighter version of the traditional sixteen-foot-long Hawaiian *olo olo*. Though the new boards resembled a coffin lid, they were shorter and allowed the rider to cut across a wave's curl at an angle, rather than simply riding it into shore on the wash.

Born on the Island of Oahu in 1883, George Freeth was the grandson of British-born William Green (Hawaii's minister of foreign affairs) and a Hawaiian woman. Growing up near Waikiki Beach, Freeth spent much of his childhood in the water. By the time he was in his late teens, Freeth is said to have "ruled the waves." The handsome young athlete was also famous throughout the Islands as a champion water-polo player, diver, and swimmer.

In 1911, Freeth headed for Southern California to surf. With his good looks and muscular body, he was a real crowd pleaser. Girls swooned, and young men wanted to be like him. It didn't take long for business tycoon and real estate developer Henry E. Huntington, to hear about the amazing young man from Hawaii who "walked on water." Huntington hired Freeth to perform his surf-riding feats in Redondo Beach—not the least of which was riding a wave while standing on his head. Huntington owned about 90 percent of the property in the beach town and believed that the surfer could attract potential land buyers to the area by offering these intriguing exhibitions twice daily.

Not only was "the Hawaiian Wonder" a hit when it came to drawing people to Mr. Huntington's fledgling seaside community, but boys from around the Southland flocked to Freeth to learn how to surf. He was happy to mentor these boys, though he foolishly did it free of charge. Money troubles would, in fact, plague George Freeth the rest of his life. And yet, he willingly shared his skills with the boys and even a few girls who idolized him.

Meanwhile, Abbot Kinney, who developed Venice Beach, took Huntington's cue and hired George to draw potential buyers to his own beachfront. Although performing his "surfing act" at both beaches required him to continually make the twelve-mile trip between Redondo and Venice, the Hawaiian needed the money to make ends meet. When he wasn't surfing, Freeth was a lifeguard, as well as a swimming and diving instructor, at various plunges (huge public swimming pools that were popular in that era). Ever the showman, he loved to demonstrate his skills on the diving board. His fancy flips and double twists became legendary.

Perhaps Freeth's greatest achievement was his innovative approach to lifeguarding. Shortly after arriving in California, he took up the cause that was nearest and dearest to his heart: revamping the entire system of water rescues. Not only did he revolutionize the lifeguards' techniques, but he personally saved hundreds of lives. Believe it or not, Freeth's concept of swimming to bathers in distress was a new one. Lifeguards, then called "lifesavers," consisted of volunteers who launched a small rescue boat into the waves and rowed to assist a drowning swimmer. By the time they reached the victim, it was usually too late. Freeth felt there should be a trained, paid work force to "guard" the beaches, especially during the crowded summer months. Instead of wasting precious time to round up volunteers and launch a boat, he believed that professional lifeguards should simply dive into the surf and swim to the victim in order to accomplish a faster rescue. The boat could be used for backup purposes. Another innovation was the "torpedo buoy," which would assist lifeguards and victims alike. Working with a friend, he developed a torpedo-shaped, floating pod—the prototype for lifesaving equipment that is still used by lifeguards today.

Within five months of his arrival in California, he was appointed as the "captain" of the newly formed "Venice Lifesaving Crew," the first professionally trained lifeguards in history. Not only did he instruct the men in the method of "rescue swimming," but Freeth taught them to utilize the strength of the rip currents to reach a swimmer in distress more quickly. Up to that point, rescue personnel, like the volunteer lifesavers on the East Coast, believed that rip currents dragged a swimmer under (hence, the term *undertow*). Freeth knew this wasn't true. He showed his pupils how to work with—instead of against—the deadly current; and to use its natural force to guide them back to shore. Now a standard practice, countless thousands of lives have been saved through the years by employing Freeth's techniques.

In December 1908, a winter storm suddenly moved into Santa Monica Bay, catching several Japanese fishing boats off guard. The small boats floundered near the breakwater, finally capsizing. When word of the accident reached Freeth, he dashed down to the Venice Pier. While dozens of men stood by helplessly watching the drama unfold, Freeth braved the churning waves and gale-force winds and dove into the frigid water. One by one, he singlehandedly rescued the fishermen. He had already saved seven men when the team he had trained in life-saving techniques saved the other three. Word about the life-and-death event spread like rapid fire throughout Venice, and thousands gathered to see George Freeth's miraculous rescues. Newspapers grabbed the story, bringing Freeth and his lifeguards into the national spotlight. As a result of his heroism, George Freeth was awarded the Congressional Gold Medal of Honor, the highest honor a civilian can receive from the U.S. government. (When he was given this award in 1910, he was only the fifth person to have received it since George Washington was so honored in 1776.)

In 1913, Freeth was hired to work at the prestigious Los Angeles Athletic Club (LAAC), where he coached numerous swimmers and divers who would go on to win world championships and Olympic competitions. Sadly, Freeth was disqualified from these competitions because he was considered a "professional." After all, he had been paid to give swimming and diving lessons. Never mind that it was the only way he could put food on his table and keep a roof over his head. The disappointment must have been overwhelming for the man who was called the best swimmer and diver in the world by his friend and protégé, Olympic gold medalist Duke Kahanamoku.

Freeth's fame as the trainer of champions spread. San Diego's movers and shakers hoped to emulate the LAAC's successes by starting their own "San Diego Rowing Club." One way to accomplish this was to hire the amazing George Freeth away from the LAAC and have him take charge of the Rowing Club's swim program. The job must have paid well, for Freeth accepted the position and moved to San Diego. Reportedly, he transformed the Rowing Club's aquatics into a winning program within the first year of his employment. But when the Rowing Club fell on hard times a short time later, they were forced to let him go.

Despite so many major successes, Freeth found himself unemployed. His financial situation was dire. With little other choice, he took a "land job." Working at the San Diego Cycle and Arms Company in downtown San Diego, he moved into a small room at the Southern Hotel. To supplement his income and continue his love affair with water sports, he worked as a swimming instructor and pool supervisor on Coronado Island during the busy summer months.

He hated his sales job, but times were tough, and the economy was slow. The "Great War" raged on in Europe, and American servicemen were losing their lives. Then, as now, San Diego was a military town. Soldiers stationed there flocked to the ocean on their days off, swimming in the all-too-often dangerous surf at Ocean Beach. As drownings soared to record numbers, local officials realized that, like their beach city neighbors to the north, they needed a team of professionally trained lifeguards. At last, George Freeth was back at the beach training San Diego's lifeguards and demonstrating his famous surfing skills.

Author F. Scott Fitzgerald once said, "Show me a hero and I'll write you a tragedy." Unfortunately, the amazing story of George Freeth, a true hero, lives up to Fitzgerald's ominous prediction.

In 1918, the Spanish influenza struck America with the ferocity of Thor's hammer. Worldwide, the epidemic claimed more than twenty million lives. Meanwhile, San Diego was particularly hard hit. It's believed that servicemen returning from the war overseas brought the virus with them. Unfortunately, Freeth lived in an inexpensive apartment building that was filled with soldiers.

In early 1919, the surfer from Hawaii who had survived raging storms and deadly rip currents fell victim to the influenza. The virile George Freeth fought with all his strength, finally succumbing on April 7, 1919, at the age of thirty-five. His ashes were returned to Hawaii, where he was buried in the Oahu Cemetery, a stone's throw away from his beloved ocean.

Today, a bronze bust of George Freeth, the man dubbed the "Father of California Surfing" and the "Father of Lifeguarding," graces the Redondo Beach Pier. It's a tribute to his surfing prowess and tireless efforts to create the Redondo Beach Lifesaving Corps, the seaside resort's first lifeguard team. Visiting surfers often drape the statue with flower leis to pay homage to one of California's forgotten heroes.

As for the popularity of surfing in Southern California, the 1959 movie *Gidget* deserves much of the credit. After seeing Sandra Dee and Moon Doggy (James Darren) riding the waves in North Malibu, thousands of young men and women, mostly teenagers (including your author), bought boards and took up the sport. Huntington Beach adopted the name "Surf City," and Pillar Point Harbor near Half Moon Bay hosts the Maverick Big Wave competition each year. Drive along California's coastline almost any morning, and you'll find surfers bobbing in the swells waiting for the next big wave to take them to shore. Thanks to the Hawaiian people and the Islands' native sons, George Freeth and Duke Kahanamoku, who came to California to surf around 1912, surfing has become almost synonymous with Southern California's culture.

Chapter 42

Hetch Hetchy: The Second Yosemite Valley

ABOUT THE SAME TIME WILLIAM MULHOLLAND TAPPED INTO THE lakes and reservoirs of Owens Valley to bring much-needed water to Southern California, conservationists began fighting a losing battle to save Hetch Hetchy, a beautiful valley in Yosemite National Park.

But national parks are protected from things like having their most luxuriant valleys dammed up and flooded. Right? So how did it happen? The root of the problem came from the overwhelming population growth in San Francisco after the discovery of gold in 1849. As the years passed and the city burst from its invisible seams, things like finding ways to provide enough water for everyone became a huge issue. Records show that by around 1900, the Spring Valley Water Company (SVWC) controlled most of the city's water supply. The SVWC began charging its customers outrageously high prices, giving local officials kickbacks to keep them quiet. The situation became intolerable.

The public voted out the city officials who had been on the dole, and the subsequent board of supervisors decided to create their own water system—one they could completely control. After examining several other possibilities, Hetch Hetchy was targeted, and the city bought up water rights in the surrounding watershed.

CONSERVATIONISTS VERSUS THE CITY
Not everyone was happy with this decision. John Muir, who is often described as the father of our national parks, called Hetch Hetchy a

"cathedral," second only in grandeur to Yosemite. Naturalists argued that if Yosemite Valley hadn't existed, then Hetch Hetchy would have never been considered for destruction. It was far too precious, too irreplaceable to be sacrificed, especially when there were other options.

Proponents disagreed. They believed the valley was expendable and that it was a logical choice. Due to its location and geology, the valley could hold the water that would drain from 459 square miles of mountain streams that normally flowed into the Tuolumne River. Because the mouth of the valley was narrow and surrounded by bedrock, it could be easily dammed. Additionally, the elevation of the valley would allow hydroelectric production below the dam.

What about other, less damaging choices, like using Lake Tahoe as a reservoir and building an aqueduct system through the Sacramento area? The possibility was considered, but when the Bay City Water Company attempted to sell some of its water rights around Lake Tahoe to San Francisco for exorbitant prices, conscientious city officials exposed the company's fraudulent activities, including collusion and payoffs. After two years of nasty court battles and the exposure of rampant graft, the project was scrubbed.

The debate really heated up after San Francisco's devastating earthquake and fire in 1906. Advocates used the illogical argument that if the city government had acted sooner, it was likely there would have been enough water to put out the fire, thus saving the city from ruin. Here's the problem with that: The earth's violent movement broke most of the water pipes in and around San Francisco, so it wouldn't have mattered how much water was available in reservoirs—they wouldn't have been able to get it to the fires.

San Francisco is located on a peninsula surrounded by salt water. Of course, salt water isn't drinkable, but many people believed it could have been used against the flames. Experts theorized that if pumps would have been constructed along the waterfront before the 1906 quake, a system could have been in place to get ocean water into hoses or buckets to put out the fires. Again, the problem was that any pipes needed for transporting the salt water into the city would have also been destroyed by the quake.

Ignoring the reality of the broken underground water pipes, many people who had initially been against damming up Hetch Hetchy now bought into the idea. A massive publicity campaign was launched claiming the absurd but emotional argument that doing so might save San Francisco from burning again in the future should there be another large earthquake.

In 1913, the U.S. Congress passed a bill allowing the project to move forward. The magnificent valley was dammed and flooded in 1923, but miles of red tape, together with lawsuits and countersuits, prevented the 186-mile-long aqueduct to be finished until 1931.

The Hetch Hetchy battle has never really ended. Many people still think the valley should be drained and allowed to return to its original state. They feel future generations deserve the preservation of California's second Yosemite.

Today, 80 percent of San Francisco's water comes from Hetch Hetchy. The water is so pure that many computer manufacturers use the aqueduct's untainted water to make their computer chips.

Another reason for keeping the reservoir intact is that the power generated by the hydroelectric plants operating along its waterways is sold for use in California's main power grid. Naturally, this creates a lot of revenue for San Francisco . . . much of which would be lost if Hetch Hetchy were emptied.

Chapter 43

Charles Hatfield: California's Rainmaker

CALIFORNIANS ARE NO STRANGERS TO DROUGHTS. DURING THE PAST two centuries, occasional droughts have been recorded in newspapers, books, and personal letters. For the most part, seasons with very little moisture occurred in the central and southern portions of the state. One of the longest and most severe droughts occurred in the early 1860s, changing the lives of countless people and the future of the state. (See the Abel Stearns story, chapter 5.) In recent years, they have become more frequent and severe, which many scientists believe is because of climate change.

If I had to choose the two most important things that shaped California, it would be gold and water. Gold brought progress and people into the state. Gold made millionaires of ordinary people. Gold built cities, bridges, and roads. On the other hand, droughts killed livestock, ruined people's lives, and devastated California's farms. Useless farm and grazing acreage often became housing developments for people moving to the Golden State. (See John Downey's story, chapter 33.)

It's easy to see why so much attention was paid to finding additional sources for supplying water to Southern Californians. By the early 1800s, dams were built to create reservoirs that would capture as much river and rainwater as possible. Still, that wasn't enough. The state's population continued to grow. The orange and lemon groves covering thousands of once-barren fields needed regular watering. Livestock grazed in lush green pastures, kept moist by irrigation canals and wells. So, when another long drought occurred, California's officials scratched their collective heads wondering what to do.

Enter Los Angeles water chief William Mulholland. He was a visionary who came up with a crazy plan. He believed an aqueduct could be built from the Sierra Nevada Mountains to Los Angeles to bring much-needed water to the area's residents and farmers. It took several years to pull off, but on November 5, 1913, a 233-mile concrete waterway opened with a roar. Some forty thousand people came from across the Southland to witness the miracle, cheering as the rush of fresh water surged through the open gates and down the chute into reservoirs in the Los Angeles suburbs.

Even Mulholland's miracle Los Angeles Aqueduct couldn't keep up with the continually increasing demand for water. Farmers planted more crops. Residents converted their yards into gardens and lawns. In the first years after the new waterway opened, everyone assumed that the lack of water was a thing of the past and that droughts would no longer be problematic. Yet, the aqueduct couldn't keep up with the huge demand, especially during periods of extreme heat. When there was little if any rain, much of Southern California was still parched.

Charles Hatfield wasn't a scientist, nor was he college educated. But he must have been exceedingly intelligent, for he figured out a concoction of chemicals that actually caused it to rain.

Born in Kansas in 1875, Hatfield had a fairly ordinary childhood. Lured by California's supposed temperate climate, his family moved to San Diego, then Los Angeles, and finally to Pasadena, where he graduated from high school. Growing up in the Southland, Hatfield would have had plenty of opportunities to see the results of the droughts. Just why he decided it was up to him to do something about the lack of rain remains a lingering question.

And yet, he made solving the drought problem his life's work. He built his first "evaporating tower" in the hills above Altadena around 1905. Mixing his cocktail of twenty-three secret ingredients in a large metal tub, Hatfield created eighteen inches of rainfall. It didn't take long for word about Hatfield's success to spread.

Advertising himself as a "moisture accelerator," he was hired by towns all over Southern California to create rain. Some contracts even specified the exact number of inches of water they wanted, and he had to provide, if he were to be paid.

Hatfield successfully performed his amazing rainmaking feat for places like Los Angeles, La Crescenta, Hemet, and various locations in the San Joaquin Valley, where much of the state's produce grew. In 1906, he went to the Yukon Territory to produce rain, but this seems to have been his one and only failure. More of his successes were written about in newspapers, including his "successful moisture-enhancing activities" in Tulare Lake, Coalinga, and Boulder Canyon where the dam on the upper Colorado River required additional water for the purpose of producing power.

He received invitations to other states and countries and was in much demand; however, he preferred to do his rainmaking work closer to home. One exception was a trip to Honduras with his assistant and brother, Paul Hatfield. It was another success, and the drought-stricken farms were happy with the results. The Hatfields' reward was $10,000 (more than $300,000 today).

In 1915, the Hatfield brothers were about to face their biggest challenge when they were hired by the San Diego City Council. They were in their fourth year of drought. The lakes and rivers were nearly dry, and people weren't getting water into their homes. The *San Diego Union* newspaper ran a story about a man who had just purchased his first indoor toilet, only to find that he couldn't flush it because of the lack of water flowing into his home.

With dead crops and livestock in what they called the worst drought in their history, San Diegans were desperate. They agreed to Charles Hatfield's price of $10,000, countering with the demand that he fill Morena Lake, which had critically low water levels, to capacity. The contract was signed, and Charles and Paul went to work.

As always, the Hatfields set up a camp site near the lake where they would assemble the tower. When they began to mix their concoction of chemicals in the metal tanks, curious ranchers watched in fascination. Eyewitness accounts related that the strange potion soon bubbled and frothed. Fumes filled the air. Then a flame was ignited, sending a white column of smoke into the air. A large cloud hovered overhead and then spread out as the smoke continued to rise. The cloud began to turn dark gray. And then they felt drops of rain. They cheered out their happiness and rode their horses back home. Many said that, by then, it rained so hard that they were drenched.

Everyone was delighted that after four long years without rain, the drought was finally over. Newspapers reported that the thirsty earth drank up the pounding rain as fast as it landed.

Days passed, and the rain continued. The lakes were filling up fast. Believing they had completed their work, the Hatfields wanted their payment. But the City Council reneged, pointing out that Morena Lake wasn't completely filled yet. That was the deal, after all.

Angry, the Hatfield brothers returned to their camp and doubled and tripled the strength of their brew. The rain continued . . . and continued. The once cracked and dry earth was saturated, and the runoff began to flood the ranches and towns. At one point, livestock and chicken houses washed down the streets, and the only way to get around was by boat.

The rain persisted. People demanded that the Hatfields make it stop. They even offered additional money if they would take down their tower and leave town. Several days later, the rain finally let up. Again, Charles Hatfield went to the City Council and demanded his payment. And again, he was told no. Hatfield's rain had caused a lot of damage, and they were holding him responsible. Furious at his treatment after there had been so much success, Hatfield warned the men that on January 27, more rain would fall, and this time it would pour.

Did Hatfield actually make more of his concoction of twenty-three secret chemicals to fulfill his warning? Or was it merely a coincidence that on January 27, the downpour was so furious and lasted so long that the flood waters swept away houses and caused the Otay Lake Dam to burst. A wall of water raced down the canyon below the dam, washing away people, livestock, domesticated animals, and buildings. At one point, the newspapers reported that more than one hundred people who lived in the region below the Otay dam were missing. Later accounts, however, related that seventeen human lives were lost, and the cost of damage to property and injured people was estimated to be in the hundreds of thousands of dollars. Who was responsible for the mayhem? Charles Hatfield, said the City Council.

Of course, Hatfield denied having anything to do with the additional deluge and still demanded payment for his work. Not only was he denied his $10,000, but he was being sued for damages. Residents of San Diego who had been victims of the floods were also suing the City Council members. The Hatfields fled to Los Angeles, where they hired a lawyer to fight the San Diegans' charges and collect his rainmaking fee.

In the end, Charles Hatfield received a small sum for a few of the expenses he incurred when he was hired for the San Diego job. The lawsuits against the City Council by San Diego residents were eventually settled, though they received a fraction of what they lost.

Charles Hatfield continued his successful rainmaking business and was never sued again. He finally retired in Glendale, California, dying in 1958. Unfortunately, he took the recipe for his famous rainmaking potion to the grave with him.

For decades, rainmaking continued to be used here and there. Open cockpit airplanes dropped the chemicals on the top of existing clouds. There are records of pilots sprinkling powdered dry ice, but that seemed to bring more snow than rain drops. Perhaps that's why they switched to using dry ice mixed with sodium chloride and silver iodide for cloud seeding.

If you think rainmaking isn't real, and that Hatfield simply got lucky, or that he had the ability to know when nature was going create rain in a certain place and at a certain time, think again. Rainmaking is still being done. And after so many decades, it seems as though the same method that Charles Hatfield developed is still in use today.

Most interesting is that Californians are finally waking up to the possibility of using rainmaking towers to help bring relief from the escalating frequency of droughts and wildfires. Of course, they're not the old-fashioned wooden towers and metal pots the Hatfields once used. Known as cloud-seeding trees, the devices stand vertically and have parallel rows of metal arms that produce the high-power cloud-seeding system. There are both fixed and mobile seeding trees emitting the mixture of silver iodide and/or sodium chloride smoke that have been installed north of Santa Barbara and in the mountains above Pasadena. The equipment is currently being installed in the Santa Ana Mountains above Orange County, the San Bernardino Mountains, the San Gabriel Mountains, near Lake Perris Lake, and close to Diamond Valley Lake. These same rainmaking methods have been successfully used in Idaho, Utah, Wyoming, and Colorado.

It seems that, suddenly, what's old is new again! Hats off to Charles Hatfield and the other pioneers who developed the original technology that could save lives and property throughout the dry areas of the world.

Chapter 44
Macfadden's Treasures

BERNARR MACFADDEN WAS HANDSOME, WELL BUILT, FAMOUS, AND RICH
. . . so rich that he buried more than $40 million in metal ammunition
boxes all over the United States. Who was Macfadden, and why did he
hide a fortune in cash?

Born in Missouri in 1868, he was originally named Bernard Mc-
Fadden. Sadly, he was orphaned at an early age and was a sickly child.
After he was adopted by a farmer, his health improved dramatically.
Physical labor, fresh air, and fresh food made a tremendous difference in

Bernarr Macfadden (1910).

the boy's life. As he grew into manhood, he discovered that, by eating a healthy diet and maintaining a rigorous exercise routine, his body and mind remained in tiptop shape.

At that time in American history, foods were often made with lard, milk was mixed with talcum powder to make it go further, and smoking cigarettes and cigars was fashionable. Macfadden's message was one of healthy eating and frequent exercise. Changing his name to Bernarr Macfadden because he thought it sounded stronger, he established a publishing empire, starting it with the launch of *Physical Culture* magazine in 1899. As time passed, he added a plethora of pulp magazines like *True Detective*, *True Romances*, *Ghost Stories*, and the movie magazine *Photoplay*. Additional magazines, like a sci-fi pulp called *Amazing Stories*, were all published under the imprint of Teck Publications. In 1911, he wrote a five-volume group of books, titled *The Encyclopedia of Physical Culture*, selling more than fifty-five thousand sets.

While he made a fortune in publishing, Macfadden's first love remained bodybuilding and all things healthy living. His investments included hotels and "healthatoriums," which offered educational programs as well as spa treatments. Macfadden opened New York City's first vegetarian restaurant, Physical Culture, in 1902, following up with another twenty vegetarian restaurants in major cities across the nation.

Known as "the Father of Physical Culture," he toured the world. After two failed marriages, Macfadden met his third wife, Mary Williamson, when he held a contest in London to find "the most perfect specimen of England's womanhood." She not only won his contest but also his heart. Like Macfadden, Mary Williamson was a health enthusiast. She was a champion swimmer and was quite attractive. During their years together, Mary Williamson Macfadden bore eight children.

They were the perfect couple, working together to increase the number of Macfadden's business ventures. He ran for mayor of New York City and U.S. senator from Florida. Finally, in 1928, he ran for president of the United States, believing that holding the highest position in America would provide him with the ability to wield more influence on the general population's health. He wrote that "robust health is not the right of a chosen few. It is free to all . . . the birthright of all." As president, he could help everyone achieve vigorous health.

Unfortunately, he lost all of the elections, and he and Mary divorced in 1946.

THE ARROWHEAD SPRINGS HOTEL AND SPA

It's no surprise that Macfadden spent a lot of time in California, where he enjoyed outdoor activities year round. Making the trip to San Bernardino, he stayed for extended periods of time at the Arrowhead Springs Hotel, a health resort in the San Bernardino Mountains. The hotel complex, named for the arrow-shaped natural rock formation on the side of the mountain, was built around the natural hot springs. The resort was frequented by California's rich and famous, including celebrities like Mary Pickford, Judy Garland, Humphrey Bogart, and later, Elizabeth Taylor, who spent her honeymoon with Nicky Hilton on the sixth floor.

During one of his many stays at the resort, Macfadden reportedly buried a box filled with cash in the nearby hills. His wife saw him sneaking away from the hotel carrying an ammunition box and a shovel. Upon his return, she later said, he only had the shovel. Upon questioning him, Macfadden told her he had buried ammunition boxes near the hotels that he owned all over America . . . just in case he ever needed cash. Emergencies could happen, and he believed he would always be able to retrieve one or more of his treasure boxes if a sudden catastrophe occurred.

After his death in 1955, his fourth wife, Johnnie Lee Macfadden, released the information about the buried money that her late husband had told her about. He had promised to make her a map of their locations but had never done so. Most people believed that Macfadden had made up the story, despite his two wives' accounts. Even his friends believed that hunting for the treasure boxes would be a waste of time. It was a fable—popular history—until one of Macfadden's ammunition boxes was uncovered by a tractor at a construction site on Long Island in 1960. It was buried on property that had once belonged to the famous bodybuilder. Inside of the metal cartridge box was $89,000 in cash, and the bills dated back to the 1930s.

By the way, if you decide to make a trip to historic Arrowhead Springs to search for Macfadden's treasure, please don't! The hotel and resort have gone through several owners since Bernarr Macfadden buried his metal box filled with cash on the grounds. The current owners are the San Manuel Band of Mission Indians. The entire resort has been undergoing a great deal of construction and will eventually include condominiums, a golf course, an equestrian center, public botanical gardens, a new conference center and much more. Could it be that Macfadden's treasure box will be exposed during some of the future construction projects on the property?

Acknowledgments

Life has been incredibly difficult for everyone during these past months because of the COVID-19 pandemic. For an author writing a book that requires massive research on an enormous number of subjects, it has truly taken an army of helpers to gather the necessary information. Libraries, museums, historical societies, universities, and literally every other institution with primary source documents were closed for well over a year. Even when they were partially opened, they were short staffed and didn't allow researchers inside. Thus, I had to get terribly creative, contacting author/historian Dr. Anne Collier to assist me with digging into as many primary online documents as possible. Thank you, Dr. Morriss, for your valuable input.

As people have gone back to work in recent months, I've finally been able to visit several previously closed venues to complete this book. Between searching the stacks of rare books and documents and using good old microfilm machines to find historic newspaper articles that weren't available online, I've been able to locate the information to resolve quite a few of the contradictions found in many of the online articles.

I wish to thank collections specialist Katy Phillips and the staff at the San Diego History Center for their assistance with numerous articles. When drafting the story of Ina Coolbrith, I was able to connect with the author who wrote her biography, Aleta George, to discuss my theories about Ina's life and her decisions. Thanks so much Ms. George for your input.

When researching the Native American tribes in California, I spoke with Dr. Kathleen Whitaker, former professor at the University of California, Los Angeles. We discussed the mistreatment of the Indigenous people by the Spanish mission system and, later, by the American immigrants. Dr. Whitaker recommended important reading materials. In addition, I wish to thank Kenneth Shoji, representative of the San Manuel Tribe of Indians in San Bernardino for his input regarding the Arrowhead Springs Resort.

Several local historians in Anza-Borrego helped considerably with the Pegleg Smith story, as did Fred Borad, an extraordinary amateur historian who is a mining history buff and an expert in California history. In addition, the Pioneers' Park Museum's historical library was good for doing research about the desert region.

The Emperor Norton Trust organization, a San Francisco group that has done extensive research about Joshua Norton, the man who proclaimed himself as the ruler of the United States and beyond, has shared a great deal of information with me.

I received help from the Monterey Historical Society and the Santa Barbara Mission regarding the stories that take place in that part of the state. Staff at the Dominguez Rancho Adobe Museum searched their archives on my behalf for material needed to put together several of the rancho-era articles. I've had assistance from the Los Angeles, Downey, and Tehachapi Historical Societies, as well as museums and libraries in San Francisco, Napa Valley, and the gold-rush era town of Sonora. A big thank you to Sonora's resident historian, Pat Perry, for her input regarding the French and Mexican miners' protests against the Foreign Miners' Tax Law.

I also wish to thank Dr. Paul Lynam, staff astronomer at the University of California/Lick Observatory, for his valuable input to the James Lick story, including sending me a photo of Lick's gravesite at the observatory. I had planned to visit the observatory, but . . . COVID.

Thanks to my friends and extraordinary fellow writers who have edited and critiqued these stories: Linda McLaughlin, Patricia Wright, Anne Farrell, Linda Prine, and Nancy Lambrecht. It truly takes a village, or at least a group of willing friends, to author a book.

Last and certainly not least, I want to include my hardworking husband, Rick. He has been assisting me with this project for months. He loves to help with research, especially when we're on the road. He proofreads my drafts and makes suggestions. He fixes my computer when it does something strange. He patiently listens when I bounce ideas off of him or have a theory about why something happened in a story, even when I go on and on and on. And he's great at finding photos and preparing them for publication. Thanks, sweetheart, for all that you've done.

Bibliography

Ball, Edward. *The Inventor and the Tycoon: A Gilded Age Murder and the Birth of Motion Pictures*. New York: Doubleday, 2013.

Beck, Warren A., and David A. Williams. *California: A History of the Golden State*. New York: Doubleday, 1972.

Bell, Horace. *On the Old West Coast: Being Further Reminiscences of a Ranger*. New York: Morrow, 1930.

———. *Reminiscences of a Ranger: Early Times in Southern California*. Los Angeles, CA: Yarnell, Caystile & Mathes, 1881.

Brewer, William H. "Up and Down California in 1860–1864." In *The Journal of William H. Brewer, Professor of Agriculture in the Sheffield Scientific School from 1864 to 1903*, edited by Francis P. Farquhar. New Haven, CT: Yales University Press, 1966.

Carr, Harry. *Los Angeles, City of Dreams*. New York: Appleton-Century, 1935.

Cleland, Robert Glass. *The Cattle on a Thousand Hills, Southern California, 1850–80*. San Marino, CA: Huntington Library, 1941.

Conway, J. D. *Monterey, Presidio, Pueblo, and Port*. Charleston, SC: Arcadia, 2003.

Cutler, M. D., and W. P. Robert. *The Mysterious Death of Jane Stanford*. Stanford, CA: Stanford University Press, 2003.

Dumke, Glenn S. *The Boom of the Eighties in Southern California*. San Marino, CA: Huntington Library, 1970.

Eaton, Margaret Holden. *Diary of a Sea Captain's Wife: Tales of Santa Cruz Island*. Santa Barbara, CA: McNally & Loftin, 1980.

George, Aleta. *Ina Coolbrith: The Bittersweet Song of California's First Poet Laureate*. N.p.: Shifting Plates, 2015.

Gossard, Gloria Hine. *Antelope Trails and Pioneer Tales: Stories of Antelope Valley and the Tehachapis*. Tehachapi, CA: Yellow Rose, 1993.

Heizer, Robert F., and Alan J. Almquist. *The Other Californians: Prejudice and Discrimination under Spain, Mexico, and the United States to 1920*. Berkeley: University of California Press, 1971.

Hillinger, Charles. *Charles Hillinger's Channel Islands*. Santa Barbara, CA: Santa Cruz Island Foundation, 1998.

Holdredge, Helen. *Firebelle Lillie: The Life and Times of Lillie Coit of San Francisco*. New York: Meredith Press, 1967.

Hurley, Richard. *California and the Civil War*. Charleston, SC: History Press, 2017.

Hsu, Hsuan L. "The Legend of Joaquin Murieta: A History of Racialized Violence." *Paris Review*, July 9, 2018. https://www.theparisreview.org/blog/2018/07/09/the-legend-of-joaquin-murieta-a-history-of-racialized-violence/.

Kroninger, Robert H. *Sarah & the Senator*. Berkeley, CA: Howell-North Books, 1964.

Lavender, David. *California: A Bicentennial History*. New York: Norton, 1976.

Levy, Jo Ann. *They Saw the Elephant: Women in the California Gold Rush*. Norman: University of Oklahoma Press, 1992.

Lord, Israel Shipman Pelton. *At the Extremity of Civilization: A Meticulously Descriptive Diary of an Illinois Physician's Journey in 1849 along the Oregon Trail to the Goldmines and Cholera of California, Thence in Two Years to Return by Boat Via Panama*. Edited by Necia Dixon Liles. Jefferson, NC: McFarland, 2000.

MacLean, Angus. *Legends of the California Bandidos*. Fresno, CA: Pioneer, 1977.

Marshall, James Wilson, and Edward Gould Buffum. "Who Grew Up with California." In *From Mexican Days to the Gold Rush: Memoirs of Marshall and Buffum*. Chicago: Lakeside, 1993.

McDowell, Don. *The Beat of the Drum: The History, Events and People of Drum Barracks, Wilmington, California*. Santa Ana, CA: Graphic, 1993.

McGroarty, John S. *California: Its History and Romance*. Los Angeles, CA: Grafton, 1911.

McWilliams, Carey. *Southern California Country: An Island on the Land*. New York: Duell, Sloan and Pearce, 1946.

Pepper, Choral. *Desert Lore of Southern California*. Chula Vista, CA: Sunbelt, 1994.

Powell, Donald M. *The Peralta Grant: James Addison Reavis and the Barony of Arizona*. Norman: University of Oklahoma Press, 1960.

Rayner, Richard. *The Associates: Four Capitalists Who Created California*. New York: Norton, 2008.

Rhodehamel, Josephine DeWitt, and Raymond Francis Wood. *Ina Coolbrith: Librarian and Laureate of California*. Provo, UT: Brigham Young University Press, 1973.

Robinson, Deidre. *Open Hands, Open Heart: The Story of Biddy Mason*. Las Vegas, NV: Sly Fox, 1998.

Robinson, W. W. *Land in California: The Story of Mission Lands, Ranchos, Squatters, Mining Claims, Railroad Grants, Land Scrip, Homesteads*. Berkeley: University of California Press, 1948.

Rohrbough, Malcolm J. *Rush to Gold: The French and the California Gold Rush, 1848–1854*. New Haven, CT: Yale University Press, 2013.

Scott, Reva. *Samuel Brannan and the Golden Fleece: A Biography*. New York: Macmillan, 1944.

Shippey, Lee. *It's an Old California Custom*. New York: Vanguard, 1948.

Smith, Dennis. *San Francisco Is Burning: The Untold Story of the 1906 Earthquake and Fires*. New York: Viking, 2005.

Starr, Kevin. *California: A History*. New York: Modern Library, 2005.

Stewart, George R. *The California Trail: An Epic with Many Heroes.* Lincoln: University of Nebraska Press, 1962.

Turner, Erin H. *It Happened in Northern California: Remarkable Events That Shaped History.* 2nd ed. Guilford, CT: TwoDot, 2016.

Williams, Jean Kinney. *Bridget "Biddy" Mason: From Slave to Businesswoman.* Minneapolis, MN: Compass Point Books, 2006.

In addition to the above-listed books, all of which are in my personal California history collection, I read newspaper articles from the time periods relating to each topic. The *California Star*, the *San Francisco Call*, and the *San Francisco Chronicle* were very helpful. Several of the smaller, local newspaper articles in the Gold Country contained sensationalized pieces and were often too biased to use as references. The *San Diego Union* provided information about a number of my topics, as did the *Los Angeles Star*, the *Southern Californian*, the *Los Angeles Daily News*, and the *Los Angeles Times*.

Index

About the Author

Colleen Adair Fliedner is an award-winning author, journalist, speaker, and historian. She began her professional career as a research historian and writer for the California State University system. Her work included researching grant projects, conducting more than one hundred oral history interviews, writing newspaper articles, appearing on radio and cable television programs, and preparing museum exhibits at several universities.

After leaving the university system, she wrote radio and TV commercials, screenplays, and hundreds of articles for newspapers, magazines, and online publications. She was a staff writer for the *Orange County Register* newspaper's online travel website and was a regular contributor for Talking Travel Radio Network based on the East Coast. Inspired by interviewing one of the first men to dive the Lusitania wreck in the 1930s, she authored *In the Shadow of War: Spies, Love & the* Lusitania, a carefully researched novel set against the background of World War I.

Colleen has authored three nonfiction books, the first of which was a work-for-hire history by Los Angeles County. Trying her hand at ghostwriting, she wrote numerous articles and two books for an internationally renowned psychologist. *Fascinating True Tales from Old California: Crooked Con Men, Eccentric Immigrants, and Fearless Females Who Shaped the Golden State* is her fourth nonfiction book.

The native Californian lives in Orange with her husband, Rick, and two adorable Pomeranians. Besides her passion for history and writing, Colleen loves doing research, traveling, sailing, and exploring new places.

Please visit her at colleenadairfliedner.com, facebook.com/colleen fliedner, or colleenfliedner.blogspot.com. Colleen's historical novel *In the Shadow of War: Spies, Love & the* Lusitania is available through bookstores or at various online booksellers. Visit her Amazon author's page at amazon.com/books-colleen-adair-fliedner.